A Hunger

with

THE SIMPLIFIED WORLD

and

THE INCOMING TIDE

Petra White was born in Adelaide in 1975 and has lived since
1998 in Melbourne, where she works as a policy adviser. Her
first book, *The Incoming Tide*, was shortlisted in the Queensland
Premier's Literary awards and the ACT Judith Wright award.
Her second, *The Simplified World*, was shortlisted in the
Adelaide Festival awards and the ACT Judith Wright award,
and shared the Grace Leven prize. Her fourth book, *Reading for
a Quiet Morning*, was published by GloriaSMH Press in 2017.

A Hunger

with

THE SIMPLIFIED WORLD
and
THE INCOMING TIDE

PETRA WHITE

JOHN LEONARD PRESS

First published 2014 by
John Leonard Press
PO Box 443, St Kilda, VIC 3182

© Petra White, 2014

Revised Edition, 2018
Reprinted, 2019, 2021, 2022

National Library of Australia
Cataloguing-in-Publication data:

White, Petra, 1975–
A hunger
ISBN: 978-0-646-98446-9
1. Title.
A 821.4

Design: Sophie Gaur
Photo: Liam Murphy
Printed and bound by Focus Print Group, Keysborough, Victoria

Set in Baskerville

This project has been assisted by the Australian Government through the
Australia Council, its arts funding and advisory body.

ACKNOWLEDGEMENTS

Poems in *A Hunger* have appeared in the *Age, The Australian, Best Australian Poems 2012* (ed. Robert Adamson) and *Best Australian Poems 2013* (ed. Lisa Gorton), *Australian Poetry Journal, Island, The Canberra Times, Australian Love Poems 2013* (Inkerman & Blunt), *Young Poets: An Australian Anthology* (John Leonard Press 2011), and *Land Before Lines* by Nicholas Walton-Healey (Hunter 2014).

I am grateful to Michelle Borzi, Paul Magee and Peter Naish for their helpful comments on the manuscript, to Jacinta Le Plastrier for her dedication in taking the manuscript to publication and to John Leonard for his attentive editing.

A Hunger was written with the support of a New Work grant from the Australia Council for the Arts.

CONTENTS

A HUNGER
(New poems 2014)

I
Thirteen Love Poems

2

THE SIMPLIFIED WORLD (2010)

The Incoming Tide (2007)

A Hunger

for
S L E R

I

Thirteen Love Poems

About Desire

Some smouldering secret, that scarcely
holds its place in our two lives.
Nothing of the ease
of established lovers
dreamt to memory.
My body still fresh with him, not yet
longing all over again.
No promises, but already
something to forfeit.
What is he that has me,
making me think he owes me his self,
the whole heat of his presence,
taking my appetite and
stripping me thin,
eating my thoughts.

For Love of Petrarch

So turtles also love and love is common, but
this is mine and no-one's ever known
it or its like – unique and coddled as
a real child whose charm no others see –

and my sudden secret smiles all day are truest
shafts of noble sunlight breaking
on the world and each poor creature
who shrivels outside all this.

And comfortable love, trying to creep
in and spread itself out and smooth off
this unbearable newness that yet
I'll bear: how hard to grip

the future tilted, *will I see you, not see you,*
will you be where I am? One crate of doubt,
and behind around before
is terrible otherness of the world that goes on,
those giant people who survive
without the whim of his attention.

Pilbara

In a dream there is a veil of water between us,
your face green with algae:
my mirror image, separate, waterlogged
in a world you trail within you.
The Aztec water goddess is you, who grew
the hearts that were thrown to her
into a prickly pear tree, each fruit
unpickable, embroiled with the spines of love.

How we climb
halfway out of ourselves to be together,
having only each other to throw to each other.
There is only the world to crack
the shell of self, the shell of us tight
and alive.

In the Pilbara,
humpy spinifex stiffens in silver light,
a silence carries us as we walk,
balanced on the thread of what binds us,
you stopping to photograph every wildflower,
your sharp crouching focus
joining up the landscape like the echo
of changed and absent spirits we can barely sense, something
charging the earth that bows up to the sky.
Of this place we know little, it holds us
as you hold me in the night, distinctly as the red kangaroo
that uninjured touched our speeding van,
the smudge of its fur on the white paint.

Meeting

And you:
so many stupid things:
I love you but slightly, I am in love but not totally.
And I am dumbly enigmatical
as a dreamt of woman,
unable to speak of love
if only to deny it.
And apart:
you start to break up a little in my mind.
The days are long clean corridors.
I grope back
to the part of my soul
undisturbed by you,
some fathom
too cold and constant for love
(if indeed I love you)
that self
here right up to death,
polishing remembered
lovers like teeth,
rinsed free of their power.

Always goodbye and hello and then goodbye again, us.
Those others poultice themselves
so close they think
they'll never part,
that love is not of distances, infinite
as white sheets spread.

Our souls: not to splosh into each other.
Our solitudes quiet sapphire green,
where we almost lose what crinkles us together.
A little bit, a little bit,
all we will admit.

Ode on Love

What he has taken of me
I don't even want back,
I don't want to want back.
This new happiness holds up
a novel mischief that waits in the near.
Why so indispensible?
Before I knew him I did not need him:
if he goes I must replace him,
as if I could. And that circling body-mashing doubt.
How he throws me
into dark and retrieves me!
And with gazes like little riffing flames inhabits me.

What does the bottom-most soul know of this –
that basin of us
concerned only with survival,
collecting residual passion
and washing clean,
shining up that bit of us
that cares nothing?

He is coasting along his own midnight.
The trapping of his breath, the only outward sign,
I devour it like meat,
as if it were him,
tenderly and watchfully in all love's creepiness.

That idea that every lover is the same,
that there's a template, a type,
that what I orbit
is an all-man man
likely to be just like my father,
many desires folded into one bright
bouquet of obsession that springs from the heart like Spring.

Love is a thing, the self's
undoing that it begs for.
He twitches out hot shivers of love he shifts away from,
exalts and voids me
with the economy of a waiter emptying a whole table with one hand.

Power to love draws the long breath from me.
Petrarch made this a joy, an Other queening distance,
love never shaken by reality, never
whittled by exchange.
I fear whatever we have will puff like a thistle.
And if not?
Mutuality, mutability, love nuanced and grappled, hard.
This seam of encounters can't peg itself down,
it is or isn't, it is high or low, a scythe swinging in, or out.

The self tries to locate him, and itself
in all the moving signifiers of love,
lover and love, meaning and feeling,
thing that says, love this one, not another.
I lie in bed scratching at the night.
Absent, his beauty
evaporates. He flickers before me,
knowable-unknowable, central lover, man-figure
skating so sweetly at the edge of a beauty.
How I hope against. How I want to know if he.
And love dares the self.
To risk what there is in hope of havocking more to risk.
Trying not to try to purloin him whole
but keep him near – to tell my heart so stupid!
The drawbridge clatters up.

The World

Oh how I enjoy sex and oh how I enjoy it   Stevie Smith

Most poems need a squeeze of grief to make them go,
but waiting for my lover
to come out of the shower is joy divided
by joy, halved, doubled again –
I lie back and my soul floats up to the ceiling,
devouring all the space,
listening to the water upstairs

rush over his body that in minutes
will rush over mine
with the speed and weight of water.
He comes down from the shower like a flock of goats
coming down from the mountain,
and he is there entire.
Love is made, a convocation.

In the room made of whiteness,
landed on the moon, the shore, the ledge,
Being expands by laps of air,
love by the kiss.
It has our scent, as my cat sniffs its owner
and a god its children, our bodies tumbling
to speak ahead of us. Just here,

the unquenched souls, their unseemly shouts,
are ravening up through time.
And a seethe of hearts,
wrenched jilted cave women,
dragon-hungry teenaged girls,
love-dishevelled bog men,
is sifting lighter than raindrops on a silk roof.

On Time

Our hope and threat the future, its silk tent
filled with all our powerless promises, waiting to billow
away to itself in the smallest wind.

How do the limbs of lovers stride
gigantic past their own future failings?
I will us not to change, to love and have loved, a circle
around us as tight as our arms, a prospect
stingless, as lovely as, oh, right now.

Selva Oscura

Hogging both time and world,
soul of another's
body, making us
as we make it,
no fighting for it,
it blasts doubt out.

Some lovers live each other out,
their love
stretches
beyond their years of beauty or keeps
their beauty, an old woman
wheeling her husband in a chair,
her love, his, flickers
through human cracks
and finds
its way to survive, alive as life, death-bound
no more than they,
sex still in them.

It is early,
we have not crossed each other,
we keep love on our dinner plates, and horror
that rips the mind out
doesn't come.
What is love
if we can kill it?
Ourselves obscure us, we obscure ourselves,
there is no distance –
love
the small chunk of light by which
I almost see you.

The Ecstasy

He is square in his suit again, the same man
in the same package, striding into the present,
meaning whatever a man can mean, a billion
years of male shoulders, male hair, male eyes,
shaking all that off, being only himself,
secure in the tight shell of his otherness,
glinting outwards and inwards,
his hand smooth as a long hill, his kindness
pocketed everywhere, let loose like singing coins,
his love, such as I know it, there in every breath,
light as a word on his lips, heavy as his body
on mine, love, about the size and shape of a man,
an embrace like the potter's hands around
the spinning clay, spinning and spinning.

The Rhapsode

Love, small morsel,
becalms the dark self, the lover
sifts, unknowingly,
through his various forms:
demon, protector, seducer;
hard to make room for him,
to make it not a sickness.

He beside me, past and future
gone, my thoughts
are the hum of a tiny machine of self,
a tiny bomb in the larger
machine of us.
What can you save me from?
Can I enter you as I enter the darkness?

The self,
that starry singularity,
it has to sit on a ledge
and wobble,
breathe into the night like a door.
This surfeit of feeling,
bricking up all the space.

Between each golden point
that isn't quite oneness
but a resting point for longing,
the dark hangs itself out again, the lover
is faceless, distant,
needing to be imagined,
invented, longed for,

love begins again and again,
further each time,
hurls itself against its absence like a wave,
and the self riding along
is hopeful as a leaf,
the tough heart flung open
to whatever may fall it.

By This Hand

In these black lines alone can our love live
beyond its rushing and its stillness, and its
whispered words that drop like water that tries
to put a dint in stone, so poets would say.
Listen. These words must preserve, and outthrive,
the crowy lines already teeming round
your eyes, and delicate redheaded beauty.
Our lust that is love, accelerated,
climbs up and up with us to age, and our
last breath's a kiss, let's bung it here, line ten.
Four more lines to kill your absence. Oh words
that cannot spring you here, come here and be
for all hungry time, and you, cold reader
of our open coffin, never say love is mortal.

Cleopatra

He engulfs the darkness, because he can.
When he says 'there is nothing to fear'
my fear rolls into a corner, inadequate. His love is the one
channel of air in a quiet dark room, the one tongue that speaks
in a carpet of mutes.

When he smiles I am like a flower
that suddenly unwilts.
His smile is a rock, leaning on another rock.
His head is a head, leaning on a neck.
He has extremities, bones and organs.
He can work and dream, be and seem.
I unfurl him like a tape measure, he unravels indefinitely.

Have you heard of such a man?
Gentle madam, no. I mean yes.
No he is not a god, his smallness wraps around me,
he croons by my cheek and breathes into my ear.
Our butterfly wings overlapping, making opaque
those scintillating patterns of our singleness.

Only sometimes does it seem to me he is a god,
and I am green with sickness, silent
with only one question: is it all right, will I live?
And his the only
yes that means yes.
So I let him be a god, while he thinks he is an ant,
crawling about his business.
He roars in the distance, little sun.
I draw towards me
the empty chair that he will sit in.

Articulation

Words fan out like green fronds, or drop
like cold grenades into my insides.
How would it be not to hear,
nor want you to speak

words that melt on me decidedly
and throw into the air the ropes
of a graspable love that doesn't stop
here or there or anywhere.

What would it say to be true. Whatever,
made in words is silence
we sleep in, having told each other
just enough, not enough, too much.

2

Ode on the End

For thou hast girded me with strength unto the battle   Psalm 18

I

A hackled old mind
crawls in its darkness,
a story-telling crab
cracking the shells of night-hours
tries to stretch itself
out of its thoughts like a person
praying for sufficiency-in-God's-eyes,

so teasingly almost possible.
All worlds must
end, begin, end,
the rap at the door you half-hear,
half-dream, will come.
A gun, a god-wrecked man.
You sit silent in your bed,

upright, two cats at your feet:
they will die at a stroke.
The curtains will fall,
the money all gurgle away,
you will live on the street
in a trolley,
in the hide of a horse.

The bed is not wood enough
to hold you up, the solid walls
are not enough.
God pulls on His shoes
to run along the pebbly shores of fear.
He will not love but save,
poor-wretched-soul-I-made-you.

In the Psalms He is outlandish and vicious
as Napoleon. He gives
you the necks of your enemies
(fear must have foes).
He draws up a battle
where perhaps there was only a soul
staring terrified at nothing

in a souped-up sky of its own.
Oh blessèd enemies!
Oh troops marching towards us —
such is the beauty of omnipotence.
Oh be at peace and sing (says God).
It is true that everyone wants to kill you,
and true you will be saved.

2

And when this dread recedes,
what will be left? Myself or another?
Everything is covered in dirt, my hands,
my face, this room.
Whatever will happen has:

Begin with love: my lover who tries to keep
me safe, take him,
then take the windows, the sunlight, the doors
that hold me.
The certainty from my hand that grips its object.
And my mind, what is left of it, this mind
hardly mine,
its words and images I don't understand, take them.

3

The fear of death:

not mine but his.
Oh that someday he
must die is
nothing my life or death
can answer to.

Gilgamesh
sat by his friend
until a worm fell out of his nose!
So I sit
by him, uncomprehending.

He is alive,
and well and will return.
But I sit,
my lifelong love
sucked up into his heart.

Fear grasps nothing,
practising its little song,
its rattle of flies,
slow shrink of mind
and heart

to a field where love can't live.
The future has passed,
the worst is here and worse,
you glut your teeth
on the tiniest bones of the banquet.

The Evening Depression Group

Depression is a river, flooding like a carpet
through and through a great hall.
Our bright pills don't stop it.
Vexatious not to be cured.
The beaming politician on TV, Zoloft-healed,
no longer needs to look into the sun
to slice its gold into his brain.

We gather here at night, each with
embarrassment of sorrow, a day all trod,
the looks of openness – so sorry, yes,
I'm still not well. The brooding retiree
who quaffs his brilliant reds
despite the meds; the fatalistic teacher
allergic to exercise who is told
For homework examine your life,
as if a life can be examined like a cloth
and that loose thread, the fatal flaw, pulled out.
We hope for the miracle,
the luminous ordinary that sings
beyond our reach.
Say there is a point in
such dark, when living should be light,
our suffering true.
Perhaps we're heroes of existence,
crawling with hope and dope.
The darkness in its tunnel makes it hard
to turn the ship of mind around,
and so the mind sludges, starless,
battling its own destroying thoughts
in a battle without will or end.

What consoles is fleeting: the elegant blue wren
just-glimpsed, soon plunges into oil, the kindly voice
cannot cut through the self's own evil.
The darkness speaks our own tongue,
truer than a music learned in infancy,
cold and safe and always home.
The world is out the window, in the white
ecstatic flowers of the magnolia,
but these are messengers
of a night that never falls, a day that never starts,
a certain way to be, that is a way to be.

Albert Road

In slow confessional afternoon workshops
the dinosaur faces plummet
through the curse of never being happy,

and the chasms of mind fall open
like books or cliffs or nonsense, with self-pity
waving like a flag in a high-up window.

We all know what we're here for
but everyone is blank as good health,
encased in an illness airless

as the very hospital. Never as whole
as the pinkish roses that flood
into the room, their scrolls of freshness

a kind of reality that prickles the eyes,
a thing to live up to, should the mind
permit, the self be allowed to walk

from imagined turmoil as if it's imagined.
Since mind can be source of all terror,
we walk outside where Spring

has crashed its way into bloom
and petals tremble on the still, dry limbs,
quiet as offerings. The mind sways in the mind.

Magnolia Tree

A mind beginning to know itself again
after a long period of hostage
to itself, its germs, its own wrong slant.
No beauty, no blooms,
but ugliness of repetition,
a world like a pill of grey,
dissolving in a glass of grey.
Never to be caught and never free,
like the sea when it is by itself,
as personal as a message, and blank and nameless.
The medicated mind begins again,
tries to imagine itself, a dance
of a dance, each step a memory,
this is me, it says, this is how I'd be,
with a notion of I as the one true self
hard as a bud, white as a bloom
that yet goes under, that cries in the night
for mysterious help.
Lowell called it murderous,
its five-day blooming. I have moved my bed
to see it where it blooms,
on every twig the white flowers open.

Feral Cow

Great Western Highway

She tap-dances on the edge of the road,
entirely her own beast. Who knows
where she sleeps, unfenced from dream
of herd, field, and farmer,
redundant on the rim
of a dayfull, then a nightfull of thunder trucks,
some carrying her kind
to the solidarity of slaughter,
skin to skin in the rattle
of metal, dull together-stench of fear.

Here she is ringed around and around by the air,
and nothing but freedom yokes her neck as she leans
to the right and the left.
Infinite cry of road,
tongue-spiking spinifex.

Morning

First the twenty-minute
ironing of the shirt.
Then the shower, like a long inhalation.
The casual shave, the tipping
of filigree auburn whiskers
in the sink. The shirt, the flick
of cufflinks.

Then the world, the bashing
of right and wrong,
tremendous space
for the daily drama.
He immaculately drives his socked
foot into shoe.

Nothing could stop him.
We are young
from minute to minute thinking
we skate on.
But it's backwards.
Our hair
flies in front of us.

People vanish,
are born.
Something
makes its indelible mark.
With enthusiasm
he greets the day
it must be said.

The Cat, Marina

She howls in the hallway
and in the bathroom.
I let her wails
inhabit me in passing
like passing Demeter on the stair, for whom
a desolation is pure
and permanent.
But intimating: let me go out, let me leap
up into the high trees
with a sparrow in my fangs,
etcetera. But she is prisoned
that she might live longer.
I listen to her howl and it becomes beautiful,
as if someone else's grief
is really cleansing
and cathartic, and
not like your own at all.
And certainly not contagious.
The cat and I
we flourish, twin fountains,
never overlapping or spilling.
I bend down my ear to her soft
unbending one
and catch each drop, her sound
that bristles on the blood
a cat alone in the hallway and the bathroom.

Memory

Our selves are for us, only we can get them right,
until they are folded away. Very hard to think
how we will fade like chalk left years on a blackboard,
how the woman who plants her feet on the floor
three and more times a night to shift her limbless daughter
in the bed that will always be too big,
will vanish despite her hard work to stay alive, the daughter too,
but we cling to what we're made of,
we cannot imagine
being made of anything else.
Love of course is in our heads,
as real as we make it, but in its pigskin gloves we feel
steeped, in it enough to last out the centuries.
There is no one ever quite as you or I, as I or you,
our never-to-be-repeated stuffs
shine out like gold from the thimble
of the gold spinner, glimmering
in that bubble our planet that is destined to be out-fired
by the ever too luminising sun – perhaps
as early as five billion years into our memory.

The Joyousness of Men

When we run together I am natively
content as a dog running beside its person.
Gladly I step out into the fresh wind
with my endless legs and swinging arms,
my dog-like pant. He running beside me
is a ball of light in his yellow jacket.
The river runs backward beside us, crinkling
and brown in the dimming air. And on the other side
somebody has a fire going. Our house
is far behind us, we are running
into the night. He sprints in great joy, he splashes
around in his soul like a duck. He waves me forward
as I slip behind. His joy, he throws to me willingly.
Love is running as if nothing can stop it,
to a grave at the end of its own possible time.
It runs and runs and says *let's run again*.

Pearl Diver

Clutch the light
as the iron hat shuts brain to silence.
And he drops wilfully forty fathoms down,
warm in his soul's fire, holding soul's gold.
The silky dark bottom he knows of old.
He selects with gloved hands, with transient breath
running up and down the lines that stream
into the living sun on deck: the many have drowned,
loot lost, heads compressed into hell.
He dodges the duck and weave
of time in fumy inspirations, here
where he gropes for livelihood, the clatter
of oyster shells like dinner plates
inaudible in the deep.

How deeply must he travel to reach home?
He'd hope for a journey
intricate as a tapestry, each step
burning off like a log that collapses in the fire, treasure
tugged from the jaws of a whale.
Tiny homes crowd in on him in the depths.
Home is the place put out of reach
for the time it takes to stay under:
the smoke of the hearth rises only in the mind,
the dog who knows his shabby shape
sleeps the long day off on its paws.

The Sound of Work

I

In their fleshfolds, in the office's
light-eating light, our lost skulls
orbit one another. We are here
to be here, reliable as mustard.
Work smoulders,
a not quite urgent urgency
– human voices quench it,
my colleagues, my brothers!

Our voices grind the air, our tales
are the tales of the world, boyfriends
shovelling backyards for love,
the self-jeers of too-skinny, too-fat.
(We know our place in the hierarchy of weight.)
With a wish that our efforts didn't slide
around forever on a shelf in space
but were noted and added to a garden of local meaning.

'The meaning of work?'
It makes us a mask, a shell,
builds us a house, it is ours.

And the department believes, as it must, it can adjust
human trajectories, beginning
with the smallest seed of birth.
What we want from work is almost love.

How our spongy brains in infancy are worlded,
forests of voices, the moving light
touching and tickling us,
the love that sets us,
never to change, forever.
We are made by what loves us:
our thought-paths grooved by the terrible
thumbs of those who try their best.
Adults, barely changeable,
we long for change, some quick
suddenness in the veins.
Here we think ourselves wasted,
stepping each day off the elevator
into a day-world farcing as whole-world,
saying never-enough-hours-in-the-day,
exhaustion almost spiritual,
change, but not sleep –
the thing given up, never to be returned
except inexactly,
already gone, already changed.

2

The familiar fears are there to greet us
morning and evening, our nameless dread
cannot go unnamed for long,
but needs a suitor, a human form, a mirror,
a bible and sceptre
to lounge with by our side, watching as we dress.

To carry self as one carries a fear, across water or sand.
Who dares hope for goodness or a safety?
That ever-oncoming:
the sack, destitution, dream job or
a lifetime left of working just like this.
And what's wrong with 'this'?

At the interviews, flint in my ear,
a peculiar pin of light cracks up, the questions
compell me into sentences, belief
in what I do, bright semblance,
gathering the work
into a bubble of dream.
I will pull all the plugs
out of my soul.

3

Our human idea of having a Self,
this bulky thing, this grandeur – it must grow
like a plant, must be watered with love, it must
have fashion, holidays, poetry, a body
gleaming with fitness, a job
that is challenging without being stressful,
it must advance, grotesque,
into some state we can regard with satisfaction
when we look back, on the slow and happy decline,
grey-nomading through the Pilbara, collecting
grandchildren as a Medusa collects heads.

4

Anxiety reigns in the office. One boss, not hated, departs
to an unimaginable otherworld,
and replacements swim the pods, will it be her, her or him?
All movements are made from within, we shimmy up
to the next level, hover there some months and then
slip back down.

5

At the meeting to generate work, which must
be conjured as water with a stick, the manager
waves her hands and refuses. Better
she says, to do nothing than let
work fly up of its own accord and roost in a high nest up there
and lay undirected eggs — we will crouch down and wait.
A new state manager, a new government,
an entirely permissible partridge.

6

The bureaucrat shines like a sword, like a word, he or she
    can do no wrong, can be sacked
for little less than murder and yet is terrified
    of error. Who more upright
than the bureaucrat's fluttering along the steady line
    of obedience, exactness,
gobbling boredom in neat bright folds? The near-guarantee
    of security is a cold
shiver of love. Governments are the wild wreckers and thrashers
    we serve politely as we can:
soul is unfurled, a picnic rug, and all life's condiments
    are propped securely thereon.
And all jobs grip like this, not one will ever circumscribe
    the jigsaw familiar, your
soul, there is no boss who'll love to hear your truest thoughts.
    And to keep yourself complete
in that world, you must learn to perform with all your guts.
    And soon you'll believe the things
you say, 'strategic delivery outcomes' will sound
    right and meaningful, your speech
will no longer grow just from the heart but from a brain
    your childhood self never dreamt of.

We have to give ourselves to something, whether it feels
    right or wrong, we flow out into
otherness, so we have something to step back from, come
    home from, return to again
next day, and if we're lucky we'll achieve things and feel
    at home in this strange world where
we can flex a power, be recognised by forces close
    to mini-gods, who in turn
one day make little gods of us. There are holes in life
    you have to find them, creeping
through the night in a breathing country town with headlights
    blazing at the dawn, moments
when soul spreads out its canopy, and fear is not near,
    and future, terror-laden,
curls back. To discover peace so strong it must belong
    to us, sing from our veins, be
sprung out from our own hearts. Who are we to give ourselves rest,
    permission to pause – as if it
were possible? Such tiny power is ours to transform
    the world with. And yet we go on,
whingeing and mumbling up the elevator, each day's
    bitter present, fixed as teeth!
Impossible to take it off us! Bright Southern
    Cross once glimpsed on holiday
in the Simpson desert: not to forget you: To stand!

A Fugitive

To blast it out of me –
I would die with the blast,
some small speck of me
remain, fearless,
cruising on every possibility,
open-eyed, without that soul
caving in, without a hundred deaths
frog-marching me along
to where and when they never say.
To blast it out of me,
the fear that chokes and cripples –
I would shoot clear of the blast
like a tiger flying from a fire,
nothing left of me for sure but heart,
body and brain,
my long long girlish limbs and teeth
once coated with fear as with plaque
now smiling in endless,
unknowable, endless ascent.

The Relic

The house-shaped Monymusk Reliquary, early Christian from about the eighth century,
National Museum of Scotland. It has been speculated that this once held a bone of St
Columba, who is credited as a founder of Christianity in Scotland; also that this was
the Brecbhennach of St Columba reputedly carried into battle by ancient Scottish armies.

The jewelled windows
sparkle like wounds,
the winking of war.
Little house,
said to have been borne
through strifes, said
to have baggaged a bone,
the numen, the gleam,

to battlers and captains
endings for whom
are distant sparks,
little as life.
The luck of a bone
in a reliquary
on neck of a man
long-lost to his family.

Deep in time,
impossible to hear him,
furrowing a field
backwards and forwards –
the charging and retreating,
greenish blades
long unpolished
breezing through flesh.

Life, said Bede,
is brief: a sparrow
flitting through
a mead hall: warmth within

is fire of the moment.
Snow outside
like the blankness
that endures.

Ungraspable stretch.
A sky sliced through
by deskbound
drivers of a droning
which cracks its
killing light
to wound a small
house, in a village

in North Wazir-
istan. At Creech
men and women
wielding the droning –
the wails, the blood,
the miniscule
unfurling deaths
infra-red

in their faces –
driving home
to houses particular
as thumb-print,
to singular families,
theirs alone,
in one-off light,
infinite love.

Truth and Beauty

Like a girl who resists yielding off
her spiritous childhood powers
and putting on the young woman's
fleshbound mystique, but coming at her is an older
self's body ever so slightly angled towards decay,
her wobblier flesh,
the way she slants,
this way or that way impossible to hold,
terrifying to this still
almost-young woman
who grabs handfuls of her youth and runs with it, a villager
gathering wet sand to bag against a flood.

Some helpful figure gallops towards her like a god,
except half of its head is missing,
or it has no head, or it is nothing but a pile of rusted armour.

It is age or it is youth,
impossible to tell:
either way there is a gape in it
that cannot be filled, a desire
for beauty, that rises and sets its thousand suns,
blinding
everyone who cannot help but look.

She watches beauty scurry along her arm,
frisking crab, flashy beetle, wounded star.
There is a shower of identical beautiful faces,
blank and luminous, young and mysterious,
perfected as the Mona Lisa, faces on which
days move and frolic
as happily as kittens in sheets.

That was her beauty,
each skerrick of which
must be given back, wrapped like a stone.

She does not grieve, she stands in her changing skin
as if it is her own.
It is neither the end nor the beginning
but the middle of her life,
the truest darkness of all.

She says, I will be radiant, my light will
swallow that net of wrinkles.

But the world, this stomaching power,
pushes her forth on the Styx of middle age.
Darkness, it whispers, hush.
You are invisible now,
except for small glimmers
in the moon's unlikeliness
and the sun's remote dailiness.

And the god
gives her a ration of remaining beauty,
tells her it must last
until the small pins of the eyes
are enfolded in the cabbage of the lids:
she must carry it carefully,
with or without a horse.
She mustn't waste it all in one smile.

Film Script

He comes for you, in restaurants, on the beach.
He knows your name, your full name,
he does not ask for identification. He has your soul
wrapped around a bullet, delicate as a profiterole.
He is your suicide, that says,
bring forward the final stars.

The man with the gun will always come,
you only have to say.
He is twin of your heart, bringer and taker
of all that is dark, he is the one
who says, at the cliff, leap —
and yet you step backwards, this time, this time,

for reasons only life can know in its fumbling,
its gasping for breath, most important.
When you are silent he says nothing, when happy
with lover or dog, he bows his head and affects to leave,
and the world opens its tranquil fleeting vistas,
it's as if he were never on his way.

Service

It's not that you aren't impeccable.
Clearly you have
an original mind. It's just – can we call you
by your first name? – something
is lacking.
The way you conducted that meeting
was quite satisfactory – you certainly
had everyone engaged
in a way that we hadn't seen around here
for quite some time.
But that was six months ago.
You haven't quite
been with us.
We've noticed you don't seem to be engaged, your work
slides off you like a ripple
and not a jet,
as we prefer. Do you need some additional support?
We know you have a starry potential,
we have seen you with a brighter brightness
in the past: why not now?
Now your brightness isn't bright enough,
your talent
claps like a clapped-out car –
is there nothing we can do to make you change?
No, you say, you are fine,
you're doing your job as best you can.
We know you're not, we know there's something
you're keeping from us, and we want it now.
Won't you let us have it?
It's just that you won't do.
So come this way please
they said,
and don't be afraid,
and there was a quiet dark room.

A Boy

c.1989

There was something he had to remember,
cycling to the shops for his mother in the morning sun.
Milk, bread, what else? The main road licked his tyres,
a bus tossed itself past like a morning paper.
His future stretched out lazy as a cat, the day at school,
that vague distant afternoon tea adulthood must be.
His brothers and sisters at home were fighting, waiting for him
to calm them with shouts of his own, his mother
was watering the garden, haloed as a spider plant in her own
mysterious silence. The scene went on forever,
nobody changed, nobody grew up.
He squinted in the sun as it bellied up into his eyes,
he felt free, and thought only vaguely
of the milk, the bread, and not at all of the car that would come,
and the driver who'd say, all she saw was light.

Girl

The same solitudes and books
plundered secretly into the night and then flung
from the window when they scared.
And the child you were, there she is
in the family video, with her twisted legs,
walking into her darkened bedroom,
her back to us, always her back to us.
She is deep in your childhood,
full of secrets, swarming with the germs
of memories, the few you might just keep.

When she walks into your adulthood, she tries
to move things around. And still believes
a little bit in God, that handiworker,
and expects you to be shocked to heaven upon death,
if not before, and she can't understand
why you haven't yet had six children,
three boys and three girls, with matching bunk-beds.
Were you going to have a career, or get married?
One thing she got right – you turned out to be an author,
though not like Enid Blyton, and that is a disappointment.

What does she want from you? Only to become you, fast,
to grapple your freedom and power. What do you want from her?
Roughly the same.

The unanxious mind

can spread as far as a sea in a world it owns, a paddock
bright in the skinkling sun, free of voices and the downward-
bearing brain. Do not envy it, for the light that shines
around its eyes is balanced upon a pinpoint; amnesia
sweetens away the menaces, the worries direct from god.
It floats like a buoy, miles from ship and shark,
it drifts like some drowned body, here to there, life to happy life,
able to smell the oatfields, hear the Delta
of Bangladesh, the minute cries of children.
What is it, this mind in the halo of its hardly thought thoughts?
But perhaps the mind can rest like a nodding daffodil.
Sailing serene as a stalk on a creek,
in a bright untroubled moment that passes without a scar.

A History of the Siege

Dark days are here.
Nothing can stop them,
they crowd like hair around the temples, everyone knows
and now we can say, at last, it is dark.
On Manus, they are walking along fine edges of themselves,
under a borrowed moon, a borrowed sun.
Nobody follows them, they would lead
only to an end of the world.
When was it darker than this?
Oh it was darker.
And the darkness is genuine,
our fingers have been dipped in it, it is felt
by all who would feel.
Where does it come from?
Us, in our masses, the massing cloud?
Our politicians, they who balance us
in their thready hands, and then plunge portions
of us and them into the pit?
Up there, a human form lies over the land.

After the Fires

Marysville, 2009

After the blazes, among the voices
that can never be silent, and voices
that were extinguished, white as possibility
the portable houses. A stubbornness
of town, its histories burned
in a truck packed ready to drive.

The bristling juvescent leaves
wrap up whole trunks, people
carry future and past in equal
or unequal parts. Vans of rental ski gear
wait on the footpath,
pointing the way to the mountain

where high-piled snow
clads branches, separates
dream from memory, heat from light,
and slides and sifts
with the screams of tobogganing children
for whom the world is snow, only snow.

THE SIMPLIFIED WORLD

Woman and Dog

A woman and a dog walked all day
beside the non-moving canal.
People who walk dogs displace themselves:

the dog sniffs and leads, harnesses
a human soul, spirit and flesh
willing or not. Its human-dog eyes

cradle the walkable world – a happy place –
a brimming here-and-yet. The canal
neither followed nor lagged behind.

There was the simplified world, on either side, green
fields and red houses. There was the little pub
they always got to.

So long they trudged, two bodies and one
soul, so many miles,
the paws began to bleed.

Little flecks of ruby blood glittered the black
rubbery pads, as if the dog was inking out
all the sadness of the woman.

And the woman, being just strong enough,
gathered up the dog (not a small one)
and carried it all the way home, wherever that was.

St Kilda Night

1

Sleepless seagulls fleer under floodlights,
they are caught like souls in light as in a net,
thoroughly winging their ways
around and through a day-dreamt freedom.
In a practice leap from love you stand
nowhere-they-can-find-me, bare feet in sand,
imagining a perfect loneliness, the soul a
self-stolen ship, breathing around the coast,
horizon-close, or sliding into darknesses
too much for you to manage, depths too deep;
and then you want a cage of light, a finite hug
to swing you back to shore. The tidy beach,
a sliver of world, blinks its toy lighthouse,
something cries, 'come home, come home'.

2

Stripped to the soul, squatting at the shoreline,
thoughts prey like sharks but never bite,
no voice inside your skull sounds right.
O listen to the tiny waves crash their hardest,
as a lap-dog yaps its loudest to be loud.
Pitched past pitch of grief: how far is that?
Easy as tides, tears ride out, words are water . . .
there is blankness wide as the long sea.
Nor be consoled nor fear. Let down your tangle
of worries, wash them in salt as wounds
like to be washed. Say you are the furthest-
out fool, lost beyond losing. Sing, and sing,
but stay where you are and wait to be found,
sleeplessly smiling (at grief!) in the floodlight.

To William Drummond at Hawthornden

O sacred solitude, divine retreat,
Choice of the prudent, envy of the great!
By the pure stream, or in the waving shade
I court fair Wisdom, that celestial maid.
There from the ways of man, laid safe ashore
I smile to hear the distant tempest roar.
There, happy, and with business unperplexed,
This life I relish and secure the next.

Edward Young: plaque at Hawthornden Castle

1

The house its own silence: walls of deep thick stone,
jammed once with books of every language,
and outside, more stone, then lyric forest,
cliffs, mossed paths, a semi-moat of Esk,
conspiring a glutful solitude.

2

I half expect the short-plod
nineteen-stone steps of Ben Jonson,
'dessembler of ill parts which raigne in him',
in the second shoes that carried him from London.
'He said to me that I was too good and simple,

3

and that oft a mans modestie made a fool
of his wit.' You wrote down all he said
(little that you said), braggings, gossip,
words that flew into the hermit's house,
caught and dried like strips of herring.

4

You lacked athletic stuff for all-night talk,
and snuffed the garrulous guest
with a bedtime taper that he ferried, still speaking,
into the swallowing dark, leaving you alone
to inspect your stranger-altered state.

5

Poems: Amorous, Funerall, Divine,
requiting privity with every-kind verse:
public tears for the public prince, then
for your private love, the terribly young
sweet woman dead before the wedding:

6

going indoors to fathom out the aspects
of a loss-devoured soul, 'laid safe ashore'
from all the world that strains to godspeed joy.
All night I hear the barn owls calling
each other, or their own insistent phantoms.

7

They are not calling me, but I am tensed,
listening to their stern goodnights,
long as sleep that Macbeth murdered
when he claimed his own gigantic solitude,
leaping onto that chunk of immortality

8

he was not allowed and could not endure.
I dream too often of some familiar corpse
that once long ago I must have killed, covered
and leapt from, into the largest life,
too filled with gifts I have not strength to use.

9

Through the window the sloping slate roof
tinges with green slime, ancient and luminous
in rain almost continuous, a conversation
we come into the midst of, as if
time does not pass but waits,

10

always out of reach and always near, overleaping
itself in the mind. My attic here like
that room of dream-recur, some sleep-discovered
nook we never knew existed, that opens
and greets us like the life I don't dare.

Older Sister

Deputy-mother of her maybe rivals,
love swings on and off.
Mary Poppins, Miss Hannigan,
spit-spot and slap-slap.

When parents say, she is shot like a comet
into adultness, to govern babies or keep
the ship of housework sailing.
Larger than adult, smaller than child,

chore-hungry and chore-fed,
a machine-child sweating at the iron.
Her fingers fly, her eyes are stone;
a ghost to herself, she body-and-soul becomes

the order that sorts the washing,
shyly perfecting the nappy's origami,
pressing the fatherly hankies
into high-piled civil squares.

On the floor, four toddlers sprawl
like dropped grenades: stilled by *Babar*,
that delicate French family of bourgeois-
monarch elephants and mint-

green apple-studded trees that float
through the screen and fill the timber house
that noses at the sky like Noah's Ark,
its cargo more than all the world.

It is like an order she has made:
four sisters, their hair still gleaming
in the braids she yanked into shape that morning.
Their future tantrums wait inside her throat,

she swallows them and keeps the peace.
The house teeters, creaks.
She slips out, climbs the voiceless apple tree,
squats quiet as a dove that ate the olive branch.

The babies drift by like clouds, their smiles
strung with cosmic spittle: she crouches,
a monster, hardened and un-hardened,
forming and re-forming,

eyes red with metamorphosis,
deep in the smell of feathers, wing-wax,
whirring breath,
she leaps from the apple tree,

lands in the kitchen, an angel,
and like four little kittens, the children
curl around her silk-slippered feet:
she pours them 'baby tea' – six sugars, all milk.

Trampolining

for Chris

The fattest eternity is childhood,
minutes stuffed with waiting
and the just-there world
deferred to an afterlife of joy
where magically we outgrow
what could tell us what to do:

we sat cross-legged on the floor, quiet
as the glad-wrapped biscuits on the supper-table,
a summer school-night boiling over
with nightmare prayers
in somebody's Adelaide livingroom,
fed air by a cooler on rollers,

our pastor bellowing at the helm,
hell's ore in his flame-cheeks.
Gorby, Reagan and Thatcher went
chasing round his head with bombs:
explode the world and bring
the roaring-back of God-the-parent!

The grown-ups stamped their thonged
and sandalled feet on the carpet:
the mortgages and what they worked for,
the chip pan bubbling every night at six,
the hand-me-downs all forced to fit:
oh take it Satan, it's all yours . . .

Any day we'd be whooshed up to heaven;
and the kids at school, their parents,
cousins, dogs,
sucked up and funnelled
into hell's gated suburb, far out
where no public transport would travel.

But my brother and I were saving up
for a trampoline: its coming required
every cent of our faith
that we might be allowed to remain
in the human world a bit longer,
to have it and jump on it: to believe

in the leaden feet sunk in the cool summer grass,
the springy canopy shooting us up
above the apple trees, all day and well into dusk,
touching heaven with our hair,
our tongues, our fingertips, then somersaulting,
shrieking and tumbling

back down into the miracle, or whatever
it was: the thing not yet taken, the present-tense,
cast off by the adults for the kids to play with.

The Weatherboard at Menzies Creek

The painted partrich lyes in every field,
*   And, for thy messe, is willing to be kill'd.*   Jonson, 'To Penshurst'

You, Peter, showing me how to build
a bonfire expertly,
miraculous as a Monet haystack,
the rubbish ordered (loved) into form:
the ten-year-old holiday farm lad
near Salisbury in Wiltshire

sixty years ago, learning in a single day
to make a rick. Apprentice at dawn,
master at noon, knowing exactly
the pitch and catch, you shrank
time into workshape, small mastery of matter
loosening the spirit:

the flame rapidly, thinly
teething up through an igloo
of ash, and smoke steadily
shuffling outwards, not sideways to neighbours
but out across the valley to the clear
space your stark cypresses guard.

The local animals aren't suiciding
into your hands. But, fluent in the semiotics
of the French butcher's window's
'beef anthology', you could use
'every part, except the hair in the ear',
almost justifying the kill.

If sick or self-engulfed when I come here,
my devils are deflected
by a stronger joy:
yours and Nóirín's who, closing seventy,
left Cardiff to marry you here. Beloved
as a woman out of Hardy,

she matches you in gusto and attack;
keeps viable this humble living.
The morning bread
swells in the truck-red aga,
your making hands
smoulder through arthritis.

The Poet at Ten

The flamingoes at the zoo were kin to her:
their long absurd pink legs . . .
She would stand before the mirror and swivel
her pigeon-toed feet a hundred-
and-eighty degrees inwards.
The knees kinked, each splayed limb
perpetually trying to walk towards the other.
She was 'pretty' but loved to be ugly.

Through the alien schoolyard she ran,
not tripping on her large feet.
Lunchtime was a wavepool of noises:
she'd strain to decipher
what sound burned in the centre of that roar.
The rule-bound games of other children
made no sense to her.
Often she roamed at large,
scowling in her platinum mop,
telling the story of herself to herself.
She was an orphan,
a brave child in wartime England, raising
her ickly baby sister in a barn.

The bullies huddled by the portable:
those she feared and didn't fear, who feared her.
She walked slowly past them,
and they rose as if hypnotised, unable to resist
aping her, wrenching their own feet
painfully inwards.

That year the surgery: the twisted femurs
were broken and straightened.
For seven weeks, on a plywood platform

tied to the wheelchair, the plastered legs
stuck out in front,
she was an island.

She loved her stigmatising pain,
four-inch hooks
neatly seamed among her bones, as if in a diagram.
On dry Autumn school-days,
at home, she wheeled herself around the garden,
a nineteenth-century invalid
coaxing the small fox terrier
to pull her chair like a team of greyhounds,
or Sit! while she read him
I Can Jump Puddles.

Motionless in bed,
under thirty hand-made cards
from children scarcely missed,
she tried to feel the bones 'knitting'.

After three months,
two operations,
she would learn to walk again,
legs transfigured,
corrected for the world.
Brown and spindly at first,
skin peeling and mottled, yellow and blue,
she would step like a baby bird.

Her near future perfect self,
a blonde Californian teenage goddess
with an effortless mastery of slang,
loped and pranced along a beach in Adelaide.

The Poem

One doesn't want to end up
like one's mother.
(One says 'end up'
as if that would be the end.)
Mother never wanted
to be like her mother,
nor did her mother nor hers . . .
You shall inherit,
the mother-mother spirit says.

Whether or not
one becomes a mother
(in the end),
mothers
exist for daughters as surely as the hills,
being both hill and hill-shadow
there with the sun,
cosying up with the night.

They will come with helpful tea,
digestive scones,
years of advice,
anxiety that unravels like intestines
to cover 60 tennis courts,
splendid as a family fleece
inscribed with gems for every worry,
every joy, every how-to-muster-love.

And no mother is wholly mother.
That is the splinter: the still-there self
longing to be other, to be whatever
new thing a child is meant to be.
I dreamt I looked after
my child-mother in the park,
marvellous little likeness
with the family violet eyes:
how foolishly she trusted me,

not knowing how I'd change her,
not seeing how my fingerprint glowed
already on her forehead.

Not being a mother,
I wonder where my spirit will go.
Perhaps into that aged blue that sometimes
is the sky.
The instant my grandmother died,
in another city,
I fell into bed with a god-splitting headache.
After learning of her death, I went outside
teeming with her secrets,
wrestling with the little mad gene-parcelled demons
that light up the brain and
harrow-vanquish the soul.

Spring

When gazing upon seas rich in dolphins, make a white
    shirt pop with statement bangles. Alone
and sad? Miu Miu's silk loungewear makes the perfect holiday
    companion. Be wild with Gucci's rock-
abilly frock, or tease in Vuitton's sky-blue hotpants,
    but harken to the mutton-meter.
When wearing the new cocoon skirts do not let your knees
    hatch their ageing butterflies. Hike up
nude tights over tucked-in sweaters and let them peek out
    from above low-riding skirts. Soften
the severity of a nuclear winter with instantly
    lifting playground brights. Oh where is last
year's snow? If your days of azure have forgotten you,
    look out for bejewelled styles, or heighten
after-hours looks with gunmetal glitter. Navy blue
    suggests intelligence, debate or
challenge. You'll love these star and dove-shaped balloons, made from
    biodegradable plastic. Lip-
stick red, French blue, sunflower yellow, psycho florals, stripes,
    polka dots: these all have springtime joy.

Ode to Coleridge

Feeling around in the human,
as if inside a sack, soul fends for itself,
fends off, prunes, cultivates,
eliminates,
makes itself up, says
'is this right?'
(and tries to be reasonably consistent)

tending itself, lurches like Sisyphus
into forwardness, backwardness,
urges itself to form a comma,
something next, next,
please move along now, please,
same again thanks,
as usual.

Those Dialogues of Soul and Body
seem bureaucratically polite.
The one complains of being chained by the other,
much like the married,
each certain of its own bounds.
What is darkness,
where does it come from?

Heavy as our fleshload,
weightless
as petals.
Here comes the train in the tunnel
(a cold blasty wind comes first and stiffens us)
will you step in front of it by some
sleepwalking whim?

Nature's anti-depressants:
some trees, blue blue blue
a three-legged dog
running as if on four,
a pet pigeon on the windowsill,
feet planted on the tired old clay of its own shit,
or a lone goat, tethered to a field it eats tidy,

skies and delicious rain
there on brain's doorstep.
Wordsworth climbed Mt Snowdon,
setting off at couching-time to meet
the climbing sun
'forehead bent Earthward, as if in opposition set
against an enemy'.

Stepping up,
grimly, grimily out of primordial self,
bearing what can't be left,
skull's cargo, hellbent thoughts.
What does he want?
To survive, a wandering human,
by some 'fit converse with the spiritual world'.

Nature his accomplice.
To climb a mountain is to climb himself.
His childhood is a looming rock,
silently glided towards
by the man remembering,
the child approaching,
then one or the other or both

oaring away in terror.
He cannot know who stole the boat.
'There was a boy',
he mutters to himself.
Nothing much happens.
The naked moon
pleases with a tricky light, the mist

rears up and writhes
its 'ocean' about his shoes.
His mind, greedy,
opens its trap.
Magician, he breathes free
the soul he keeps chained
like an animal inside him.

Frames

The bright rosy faces of those people –
inhabiting their place, the moment
without fear,
as if they lived in hives
of love continuous
as gas hotwater, and flowed

through seamless days and had
no reason to suspect themselves.
Solid worlds,
where solid things are good.
The faces sheet,
the eyes look past.

How to keep hold of a self
so frangible, so often breaking up
and coming back together,
a living mosaic,
a small piece of wood,
a hide-house of hair.

*

Flying over the old leather surface of the sea:
changing and not-changing,
a slow holding-together
of desolate parts, thoughts rapid
as geckoes flicking
in and out of the mind's story.

Density of clouds,
boiling crystal,
something rumbling
and beginning
in the one silence, the human engine
in the plane's roar.

The unmatched spines of hills
spread like cattle.
You unpick the bones
of a stream, then a river,
widely, bluely
opening into larger blues, layered in
an immensity of air.

*

A heart-unfurling peace:
the loudness
and largeness of the waves,
and the eye-breaking brightness –
all that there is!

In order to stem the slow internal bleeding
of grief, or illness,
the thing
that thieves away silence –
fall down here like a shipwreck,

you ungraspable soul:
for you truth changes
like sand underfoot,
this moment a coffin,
the next a hope that sails.

A lizard squeezes
through the long grasses;
briefly its head,
golden, fat, pulsating
in gentle riveted joy.

All the world rivets the mind:
do not wrest yourself
from this, the day,
intent as a story to be learned,
while there is time.

Notes for the Time Being

How many sonnets must we write
before the great gong sounds in Heaven?

Peter Porter, 'Whereof We Cannot Speak'

Relieved like a criminal
at last apprehended
and tricked out of daylight.
Will I be you again?

Too much freedom
is not enough.
How large or small the world
where time fits.

Terrible thing a head
from which no thought escapes.
As the world said
good-bye to you

it grew small and glazy,
a thing seen beneath tears
as when a child says good-bye
to a too-much-trouble pet.

*

Soul frees itself
(from something),
or tries to imagine
it gone, the heavy –

still carrying
what's precious
– the gold, the old –
and the fuse hope.
Thrown into light, thrown into dark,
etc. Where does illness live,
what does it want?
And sits before the Sybil,

begging for speech.
Describe your fear.
How do you feel out of 10?
Out of 9?

*

Soul is confused, sad for no reason,
can't remember;
sits in her chair and stares
like someone much older
who'll never again remember.

Weeps, as if out of the corner
of humanity's loose mouth;
her tears are lost coins, spilling down
the loud spiral of that machine,
somewhere in eternity, that codes them:

Grief 1, Grief 2, and
how unusual: Griefs 11 and 19.
And sometimes, of course, there is joy,
also for no reason – here you ask
what has reason got to do with it? –

For the Moon

Alpacas

The cria had been born early, the owner not yet
aware, not there to supervise, inspect,
to be farmer or man. The cria was there,

new, staggering, abrupt;
its comprehension already filled-up with a universe,
this fleece-producing field bordered by a driveway,

where elders were standing around, teaching it stillness:
mother blood and awe, the others half-looking
over their shoulders, seeming nonchalantly private.

Visit

i.m. B.L., SJ

Visiting your brother, the priest, in hospital,
he may be dying, coughing blood, they
don't know why. His legs leak, he has lost jolly fat.
Alone, half naked in the public ward,
he greets us: one dainty leg drawn over the other,
face luminous, eyes lively;
not saying 'why this suffering',
just present, like a character in a fresco,
man with blood bucket. Humanly
getting-on-with-it, he hacks into the stainless
steel and shows us 'rather red as you can see'.

Beauty

I stepped into Beauty, this was it: islands,
mountains, water, clouds and sky.
Not the street in blossom

or autumn leaf, or the dog in winter leaping
at the window, but Beauty raging
because we knew it to be.

Then I slipped back to the usual, the time-too-fast,
the life I crave to love more truly
than any mountain could surmise.

The Couple who Own the Lebanese Café

Each morning except Tuesday for twenty years he rises
at four to go to the market.
Each day they are there in their shop,
she, impossibly sexy in loud tight dresses,
casually turning the skewers,
he outside, soberly drinking
with the regulars.

Behind the counter they dance around each other,
as if they are building and re-building up love
that washes away each night
as love must, falling under the tide, dissolving
in the heart of the farthest star, to be reborn
entirely through human effort,
the smallest gestures, the brightest capsicums.

Debtor's Prison

Do not look for the future, it is gone,
tossed away clean as a wish-bone
over the shining shoulder of a dragon
with oh! the silver clogs we now repent,
those credit cards we spent to space like rockets:
the past tense will heavy our shallow pockets.

Same old same old. And the snark present-tense
cares only for itself and will not cleanse
out our wounds like a loving fellow cat.
Use what strength you can to sorry-smile
at tomorrow's better woman, who all the while
flexes her teeth and can't help but regret you.

Holiday

*Behold, I shew you a mystery; We shall not all sleep, but we
shall all be changed . . .*   I Corinthians 15:51

for Kate

We stride into the white waves like kings.
We who demand perfection
of ourselves and the world, we proclaim
the height of the spray to be flawless,
this sky immortal.

We surge on the breast of life as it should be,
no rocks or seaweed or monsters,
our glad heads thrown about,
luminous and singing. Later we talk
of what must be repaired: the severed self,

its open wires of longing,
its childish hand grasping for care.

Description of a Ritual

Freeling Cemetery, South Australia — i.m. Valda Ince, 1934–2008

Life a mere flash, or flesh —
coins-as-headlights winking in the daylight,
and we are all in Charon's dinghy.
Our creeping vehicles fog up
with family gossip: then our car-sized groups
dissolve into a clan, semi-strangers with like faces,
attending the secular comforts of religion.
Nobody is damned or redeemed.

We're flowers that open and shut, we endure
shiftily in memory. And the dead
have afterlife in local habitation and a name.
This place she chose for herself, the burial
modelled on her friend's, last Winter — the cemetery
fringed with cypresses and a caravan park,
its modest frontier of headstones
facing out miles of unborn suburbs.

Her graveside is formal as a picnic, a row of chairs
along the edge for those who will most
weep, her grandmother-daughters,
seeding her down with tears
a water-holding grave can hold. They are bowed
by afterlove that the dead, leaving the world's cold,
drape around the living like a coat,
but the sons and grandsons, flanked behind them,

bearded and pony-tailed,
are inscrutable as the Pictish ancestors
we may or may not share. Green slithering hoists
unravelling to its fathom, its this-far-no-further,
the coffin goes one finite down,
and a pungent, non-descript hell
remains above, digesting love-never-enough,
embryo losses hatching in the open air.

Adopted to child a marriage, she
knitted herself into new blood,
then seven came by birth.
She was their principal Sister from the elsewhere
of First, keeper of all goodness and terror.
Her toddler brothers shadowed her to school,
she smuggled them in and fed them
what she knew of the world.

And in death she is adopted again, the first
(as an adult) to die. Her ageing brothers and sisters
carry and bury her, their own in words of stone,
and scattered in anecdotes.
How glad she would be to zip away,
gripping the wheel with hungry speed
as my father does, for once at peace with GPS,
the slightly-rights and worldly lefts.

Blue Above the Chimneys

Christine Marion Fraser's
autobiography, I found
in a second-hand bookshop
in Kelvinbridge, Glasgow.
Christine's father, as my aunt
recently discovered,
was my great-grandfather,
who had had a second family
in his sixties: none of our
business, perhaps.
I grew up knowing nothing
much about his son, my dead
grandfather, Alexander. They say he was tall,
and liked to draw and write stories,
was a bully and a drinker
who often fell apart.
He left Glasgow in his youth,
settled in Adelaide, never
returned to visit, and in 1960 died young
of a heart-attack, in Melbourne,
leaving seven children and a wife.
Around the same time,
his father, John Fraser, at sixty or so,
a widower, married a widow:
they had five children,
Christine the eldest, and they lived
in near poverty, in a stark grey tenement.
He worked in a Glasgow shipyard,
drank, and could be violent,
gruff, steely, also tender.
Christine describes him

as bird: 'his iron-grey head
sticking out from our kitchen
window one flight up, his eagle eyes
raking through the tumbling throng
in a search for his brood of four'.
His hands were 'horny' and 'hard'.
His wife, Evelyn, died at fifty-two
of 'weariness', and he shortly after,
at eighty-one, of grief for her.

    In Glasgow, my eagle-eyes
raked through the streets
(nothing 'tumbling', no throng –
quiet, slow-curving crescents).
In so many Scottish faces and voices,
a toughness, a cheerful grimness,
as with my relatives or me.
But there was no-one in this city
that I knew, and I was happy not to know
who I was related to.
There must be a point when family,
foreign as ancestors,
is not family: all the threads
of distance and doubleness let go
into a human larger narrative.

Christine's world overlaps
mine and my Aunt's, mainly for the early story
of how my grandfather may have been
if he was anything like his father.

Imagination

The air was always cramped with miracles.
The church, or 'assembly' would gather
in a grand old theatre: the pastors
emerging one by one from deep red curtains
to take their seven seats onstage,
a chorus line of suited legs.
My family were new recruits (I was seven)
snapped from a life of sin to cancel beer
and swim in the crowd of converts
who called each other 'Brother'
and 'Sister', 'Aunty' and 'Uncle'
– the lie kept me spellbound.

There were tales of cancer
diminished to a pea by prayer,
addicts dropping their needles and singing.
Proof of God was always needed
by believers. Miracles
made life worth having, each subject struck
by God as if by lightning.
Heaven delayed, we roamed together
for sundry salvagable souls
in the wrecked world's wreck.
My ten-year-old friend Sarah
got a cancer that was stronger

than faith: her leg with its large knot
was amputated. The night before that
the whole assembly shouted
and prayed for the cancer to die,
her leg to be saved. Oblivious
to a thousand prayers preying on her leg,
pre-operative, she was deep in a scarcely
imaginable childhood bravery, imagining
how she'd learn to walk again,
her artificial leg thrown sideways and forth
with each dancing step, a survivor,
a jaunty jagged figure in brazen health.

The Gone

We turn them to stone when they go.
(It is always them and us
with the dead.)
They have mostly been dead
too long to still be mourned.
The tilting graves are exhibitions
built up inside: here are parents,
children and grandchildren,
flat-packed into the present tense *here lie*
and the single past tense of the headstone.
They have slipped beyond family
and twinkle anonymously
in the magical DNA that lies
about like powder at the edge of things.
But our own dead are everywhere.
Closing our eyes at night,
we imagine ourselves like them,
perhaps in a zone where forever
we might freeze, or a sea
or river we swim for all durations.
They tour that multiplex
of wherever-we-think-them-to-be:
shadowing us to work, leaping onto the bus,
standing by the filing cabinet, chatting.
Something about existence
insists on presence.
The dead, surely they just want life again,
and it is there:
haunting them up to their eaves,
clinging to their hands like ropes of ghost-cloth,
vexing their spoon drawers,
blitzing their screens with images.

The Orchardist

Renmark, South Australia (Riverland)

In the bitten dusk, his lemons
gleamed their own light, too much, too rich for harvest.
He was blacklisted, we later learned, for cheating workers,
the wretched flesh, unpredictable as weather,
he hated to need. Two kids aged 9 and 10 had spidered
words in Romanian on the bedroom wall
in the derelict fruitpickers' house.

At night we walked the river, following its curves
that wound us out to where a redgum
stood marooned at water's edge, fossilised in thirst;
a sliver of silver still flashing
in the cavernous bed, eluding, for now,
the underground stealthwork of pipes tugging the river
out of itself, into the ticking sprinklers.

At dawn we were into the fragrant avenues of citrus,
dreamily caught in the strangeness of labour.
Throwing our ladders on the mass of a laden tree,
lunging blind into the leaves, we learned
by hand instead of heart; our finger-muscles
rippling up, reaching and grabbing, tearing the fruit
from its branch as if from a painting.

All day the farmer circled on his tractor, mad as a bull-rider,
lurching on thick dry mud-tracks braided yesterday
and yesterday, shouting *Truck coming tomorrow!*
as if to say, *The end of the world!* On our last day
his neighbours mushroomed in the avenues
to help; sauntering past us, he glinted in defiance: *I hire
a million dollars and grow this up from nothing!*

24th Floor

The desk is pushed up facing the window.
Sleepless lights, dry voices, partitions shielding none.
Then silence after 5,

an absurd desire to seize the day, too late.
Invisible the turtley Dandenongs,
ninety-three minutes of cruel traffic hence,

never not there, never closer:
the desk like a plane that doesn't land,
the day only pretending to end.

I hear, still, a colleague's bitter curses, tirelessly
at the system's recurring red letters saying 'Error'
– human passion authentic as phlegm,

clinging to the air's contagions and my own
festering cold, a migrant
from that desk over there, proof of connection.

The cheap building rattles with winter
storming the glassy streets below,
all wind and little rain, and more than weather:

something else, some dampness of the mind
that spreads and seals a comforting alienation.
The unfelt rain a fury of scratches on silver.

Second Ode

Wordsworth is far from the grave
of his daughter. Surprised by joy –
not of his being: a transport;
something carries him.

From A to B, just fleetingly,
out of grief's bog,
he doubles, triples, whirls on the spot:
joy, sorrow at joy that can't be shared,

guilt at joy's split-second song.
Oh heart, that some
vicissitude has found:
we have climbed this far, and where next?

New Year's Eve

Our picnic on the beach pinned down by food.
A wind-dark sea
is all but people-swept, just an incandescent white-
sailed boat stealthing outwards:
out to where, to where?
Where weather comes from:
always from 'out there', where everything new is from.
The boat is gliding swiftly out, its sails a steeple,
it means to change, to come back new,
its people cheer-filling its sails.
At the tear in the year,
the storm getting closer, the hungry new year
furrowing in, the boat forging out, it happens:
the dark needling rain comes sideways,
we see the sailboat steadfastly sailless in the gale
sailing back to our shared shore.

THE INCOMING TIDE

Planting

So he gave you the tobacco plants, seedlings,
and you planted them behind the house
you half-lived in. He was nobody,
friend of a stranger's friend. But he
gave you the seedlings and you pressed them
just lightly in the soil, before night
fell into rain, heavier, darker, greener
than the tiny sound or hair-line root
that might have flared into a moment's light
as you lay still. When the rain
stopped, the eaves and over-burdened gums
let fall their water, a long, unbounded echo
that welled into morning. The garden gurgled,
the plants drowned, the sound was yours all night.

Sister

for Ellie

Her axolotl dips in his cage of water,
his polite uneraseable smile swanning
him upwards, the rubbery, tail-heavy dragon's
body tilting down. The tiny golden
Aztec eyes, blind, lidlessly slumber
through the waters of his kitchen aquarium
like never-quite-sinking coins, or beacons adrift,
with scarcely the ghost of a reference

to the mythical flicker of the salamander
he genetically sidesteps, even surpasses
by his own more modern brand of indestructible
– his species kept alive by scientists
for a keen ability to regenerate:
his limbs, if lost, will soon resprout; even
some parts of the brain, if chewed off
by a sibling, grow back. Only the crude lungs

connect him to a world outside him;
once a day he noses the surface and breathes –
then free-falls back down into depths of swirling
grit. Ever larval, babyish red ragged
gills fronding wildly round a blunt head,
sealed by water in the jewel of himself,
he survived the pumping of his stomach
after gutsing seven lumps of gravel.

Descendant of the Aztec dog-god
Xolotl, who with mangled hands and feet
guided the dead to heaven, his once trans-
lucent form refuses catastrophe; more
than the ailing tabby, the timorous
and watchful high-heeled dog, or the rented
fireprone house, he guards our dangerous
childhood pledge to never change.

Pacific Gulls

Shallow Cove

The gulls are coming in, nosing their way down
from clifftops in planing half-circles that span
whole corners of the beach, widening and lowering
where others already are, hovering there,
then tucking feet, assembling to face the incoming tide.

This is their place, they can die here, like the one that lies
in the reeds, its orange-and-red geometrical beak
jutting upwards, hooked on air,
splintering out, cosmic sift,

other identical beaks smashing clams and sea-urchins
on the rocks all day, their harsh, sky-scraping cries
brought home by rain and wind. Dead and alive,
by foot, beak, feather, guts, they occupy,
as if there were no edges or ends.

Ricketts Point

A slim girl playing by herself in the shallows,
like someone who's never been to the beach before
and suddenly marvels at how the world
tips open to broad deep space, not fearsome.
Seawater cool as milk intimately swirling her.
Sand hospitably absorbing and releasing her feet,
her mounting dance of being, luminously alone
on the sea's hearth, its hissing welcome mat.
Two bearded men, perhaps her father and uncle,
identical as Kafka's lodgers, further out in the waves.
A third man out there with them hurls them a ball;
they miss and laugh repeatedly, rolling like seals
under the waves and up again, under and over
their joy that won't stay under, and mirrors and magnifies
the separate joy of the girl, her not-to-be-tested trust.
Smiling at strangers perched on their towels
who can't help watching her, and smile back as if her world,
scribbled and wiped from soaked and pre-soaked shore
and flung from her hands in effortless wave-sprays,
was large or real enough to include them.

One Wall Painted Yellow for Calm

Job Network, 2004

And should there be a fire, we simply go out
    this door to the left
up the stairs and out the door you came in, but
    if for some reason
that door is blocked then don't worry we go back
    along the hallway
and then down to the end where another door
    swings through to the street.
Where we can meet and I'll be holding this list
    of all your names to
check off against you and everything's fine, yeah?
    Breathe out. Consider
simply that your hitherto cold, doubt-riddled
    Quest-to-find-a-Job
has gained a sudden cosiness. Oh I am
    cognisant of course
you're not here by choice. Some of you might think
    that you have other
things-to-do or lives-to-lead – that's natural and
    all I can say is
it will pass. I know you're probably thinking
    I'm just some geezer
who'd be like totally unemployed, if not
    for the unemployed –
so we're all in this together. I always say,
    we are each of us
individuals, to whom anything can happen.
    Last week I had a chap
determined to be an Ambassador and
    spoke six languages.

I said cool, you follow your dream. Only bear
    in mind that dreams can
bend like starlight. Then a tailor rang me up,
    quite sorely in need
of an apprentice and located quite near
    where Pete lived. I thought,
I'll just offer it to him on the offchance.
    And off like a shot,
he was working the very next day. Just being
    in this room he found
himself a life. It's the life's the thing – the dream's
    a vapour waiting
to be coughed into any shape. I know this
    room isn't pleasant
– someone said it's like being in hospital! –
    but think of these walls
as holding your chances up. It's ok to
    yawn. Standing up here
I can't get a true sense of the temperature;
    please sing if too hot.
And when you leave it's natural for me to say
    'see you tomorrow'
or 'have a good weekend' but – and I do mean
    this in a good way –
I hope you find what's looking for you, and the
    future will take you
with swift undeniable closure. I won't say
    see you tomorrow.

Grave

On the headstone's frame, her photo
in the veiny case
blooms and swells. Lines of weather
or sight, scratch across
her double-breasted coat, crab at her eyes
but her cheeks are flesh, the face
visible, a child's gazing
up at God or the camera. Her coat
all buttoned and sealed up.
A child, finished or not.
A thought, fingered in the pocket, barely
formed before the lens flashed her
out of time, and parents
buried her with prayers
for her future – and roses coy
toss out a careless petal,
a notice of resurrection,
vanish in a cough
of their own dust. She's left
to rot in peace.

She hesitates. Turns slowly
in her grave and cannot
turn back. Above herself, she records
the sun's persistent angle. Her blue eye
stares out the stone. What does God see?
Passing, she draws me in, and I stumble
as if in suddenly loose soil. Her seeing seeps
from its frames and breathes the visible air.

Even her faith must return to its element.
There was salvation: she was prayered-in
by a foliage of tongues,
that murmured with the beginnings
of prophecy, rustling swaying bodies,
shielded and made naked by their own closed eyes.
An old lady etched in sudden light,
her tongue knotting inside the cheek,
a prayer working up and down her face
like treadled thread; and on the platform,
above a packed array of shoulders, cuffs,
the elbowy pastor, smoothing his tattered grey suit
(waist-deep in ocean he baptised the cripple
who rose from his chair, legs growing back).
The hot sun, an uninvited sign,
crashed through the blood-red curtains
and circled with the dust. Then voices
as if from other bodies, other times,
burst out in a wordless torrent,
sailing them up above
that sin-sacked world:
We Have Built Our Ark!

She saw not the heavens but their heads
gleaming with the bulbs of new stories,
a sudden sea, surging round Noah's prow –
and her life, all bundled in repentant prayer
passing his eye like a fleck of dust
or slant of rain, brief unsteerer.

Did Noah never snarl the hair
of a giraffe, grizzle for the world?
Cowled in a wooden womb, the species;
Shem and Ham and Japheth and unnamed wives.
Was it peaceful at the helm?
Or was his weathered, wind-slapped skull
still poked and mocked by people no longer real?
– who would not heed the flood
that seeped into their very rooms,
warped their wallpapers, unsettled
their dinner plates and floated their carrots away;
invaded their speaking mouths, inching above
the windows of their aquarium houses
– as anything but rain, brought on
by a hidden cloud, from which
like swimming dogs they ran,
in mortal fear of *Weather.*
Not even a little boy
stopped to believe he might rise, his eyes
constitute a hole, through which
whole trees could be withdrawn, histories
and deeds unravelled
within his seeing, to the needle-point
of never-having-been. That his memory too
would simultaneously vanish, and he
touch light by being light, with hands
more music than any music they could play.
God's burn, sunlight veining a leaf:

could she, with an accidental turn
towards a world imaginable to Him,
shake Him with a wash of finite gaze?
With priseable cracks, her picture.

A young and unrebuked stone,
flowerless in a fraternity of weeds,
shouldering the wind-tunnel gasps
and sound-emptying bells of Lygon Street trams,
among blackbirds and frail, pink-clad widows
who bend, effortlessly between prayer
and three-cornered conversation.
Stubborn upright,
a whispering wall, the unyielding vocal echo
of one who shouts though inaudible in the surge,
Get Thee Back, God! Thou Hast Made
Thy Bed, Now Lie In It!

But her silence grows, her
forgetting is steep. In a moment, her moment
will come. All He needs to recall her is a flash
of light, a thought, barely formed.

Southbank

I

When the system crashes, and the screens,
and palm-hugged
beaches that saved them,
crinkle out
the office tilts like a ship.
Small murmurs
of surprise, voices like children
who'd been playing in the shade,
shocked by sunlight,
flurry and subside.
The thermostat
shudders its seasons
of freeze and sweat;
furry square windows
seal in the boredom (a little man,
I've begun to suspect,
tweaks the levels each hour).

The quiet settles, doing nothing
settles, the sister of work.

The mind rises from its bubble,
and eyes unscrew from their
mid-screen float.
You rise and walk down the hall
like someone freed:
the woman who comes early
to work late sits darkly in her glass
as if waiting for a traffic light
to change, or an eclipse
in which nothing
is remembered, to end.

Time with nothing to smother it
creeps up like a mist from the river
and cuddles the office friendships,
emails caught mid-send, the million strands
of life rich as Pompeii.
Three women whisper in the kitchen.
Somebody laughs, someone else
cracks his finger joints.
Nobody stands and declares
All this was a dream, well, thank you, I'm off now!
Why should they? Over there a man,
pacing in his pod, has a deadline
as real to him as his wife.

So it starts again, you slip back
to your chair, the hard-drives
rev up in chorus, their
engines mingling with the rise-again joy
of humans working
with our without-purpose:
happy if we remember
whatever ten minutes before
fulfilled and/or consumed us.

2

Alchemies,
time into money
that flits through our hands
faster than a solitary wren, faster than time;
houses, children, cars, dogs –
the self's empire of proof,
menagerie of power, *I am here.*

Our time sold not hired,
our names as simulacra
show us up in our absence
on semi-partitions, brass-plated.
We forget, like monks, and serve
an abstract we must
not care too much for.

A prison of light, it dissolves
in the mind as you fork
home through traffic,
each former workplace that had you once
a sketchy edifice of neon,
you can't quite remember
what was I there?

Our little day is rounded with
a commute and a sleep
a spend and a keep.

3

I am pleased to announce that *Wayne Loy*
    joins the *Networks &*
Infrastructure Team to give cover
    until Jill returns
from maternity leave. Wayne reports
    to me alongside
Jill, April, and Tarquin Dobrowski
    (in Sydney). Many
of you know Wayne already in his
    contract capacity;
I'm sure you'll agree that he's proved both
    able and helpful.
I welcome him to the team and ask
    your patience while he
learns many facets of his new role.

4

Out there they are bombed-to-nothing,
filed to one-sidedness, starved,
ejected by outrageous floods,
earthquakes with no sense
of timing or propriety,
but often a preference
for children in rickety schools.
Ears press down to speaking debris.
Is work a 'necessary evil'?
Office workers lose approximately
two hours daily
reading news websites, ebaying,
chewing up email, fending off
fidgety distracted colleagues, scoffing
pink and yellow cupcakes.

5

Following on from the death of Bob Smithson
last Monday, Smithson employees world-
wide have been escalating messages of
sympathy, prayers and condolences, all of which
are moving and on a global basis I thank you personally.

Aptly described by one employee as 'an icon of integrity, leadership,
philanthropy and business acumen', Bob Smithson will be
sadly missed. The family are currently progressing options
for a public honouring of Bob. A nine-minute webcast
of the funeral will stream to your inboxes on Thursday.

6

The receptionist
who chills everyone is suddenly
being terribly nice, baking cakes, everyone
is suspicious –

7

What privilege
to put on a suit, walk upright –
since childhood
shaping ourselves
to be in the world: flourish up and work,
as the parents, the toaster,
house not falling down,
the family itself spun whole by years
of making, desires tamed and made to flow
in single file.
Each day a threat
by human rage,
a mother in the garden
smashing the family pottery –
and Heidegger said
only when things break down do we begin to see.

8

The paramedics come into the cafe –
jaunty in their blue and red uniforms, their solid black
police boots. Two espresso, their phones on the table,
antennae like the half-listening ear of a dog, they
dangle from the emergency that hasn't
yet happened, that is less than a hum in fine air, she
with bright auburn hair, laughing.
He sits back, arms folded, legs outstretched like a man
who has the whole morning newspaper before him.

9

Skill tugs at the muscles, drives
the bones, the mind keen,
the child perfecting her scales,
blocking the din.

The child understands the adults,
ignores them, thinks she is innocent,
making herself. She reads
the dictionary, the bible,
dinnerplates of language,
at school dwarfs herself
with long words.
Priggish, pigeon-toed,
she walks her book in the schoolyard, stalks
blind through netball.

The thing we work for (rarely
work for its own sake) vanishes;
work persists, then too is lost:
the black hole of energy burns
through hands and minds.

A heaven somewhere,
a palm tree, a beach, a child, an apartment,
the quiet hum of one's power
of being that flexes around days,
carries futures, saying
world is made for me as I make it:
small enough to garden by hand, large
enough to outscope me,
for I must not lose surprise: this illusion
I with my labour can sustain.

10

Elevators dim-lit, dark-polished all day
by a woman from Bosnia, cheerful as Sisyphus,

who greets you with a suicidal smile, her trolley
of rank cleaning products makes her sneeze,

fills her eyes with red wires; she apologises, grins.
She scales her never-done job, a moonwalker

trailing her cargo through the semi-mirrored
obsidian tangle of offices, herself glowing back at her.

You ride up with her, pin-prick halogen lights,
mirrored walls you vanish into, she polishes.

II

Through a fifth-floor window you can watch
the new tallest building in Melbourne being built
one gold brick at a time.

The city sprawls
in late-mid-morning, the workers
housed inside their work: time
is everywhere engaged.

The office a portal,
point of stillness from which the world extends;
a kind of sublime.

On the seventh floor the company director
muses on his monthly
email to all staff.
Three slabs of sky behind him, he faces
the fourth wall.
The football season is upon us
and business too progresses . . .

Highway

Moto

His movements are rectangular as a dog's
that half stands and turns in sleep, then drops again,
knocking whatever is there. He eats all the oranges,
then paws the oat-sack, cries *I've still got opium in me!*

Then sits silent, glinting below the brim of himself,
the window behind him teeming with road that flashes
like endless possibility; reels of his dodgy past, and present
and elsewhere. He refuses to hug the others, who ever-hug,

or change his clothes that drag like oilskins,
skins of dreadful baggage. Nobody pretends to love him,
nobody wants to keep him. See, not a day into our journey,
they're negotiating leaving him here, in this scarcely

identified, scarcely inhabited town. We watch from in the van
as two of our men try to give him back his petrol money.
He staggers, looks lost, and the four other vans creep round
as if to shield the scene from the wind,

or the gods. But we can't throw him out, he is our fool, our thing
of darkness. So they throw him back in, and the 'tribe' drives on.
That night he cooks us burnt potatoes, parodies Tai Chi,
severs our weedy pre-dinner song with his OM! like a war cry.

Eucla, 6 am

Willow the four-year old blond boy
sleeping like an egg
in the dunes that dip,
compressing the desert and
hiding the shallow
weedy lap of the sea.
Cecilia his mother,
wailing and staggering
in the hot, crystalline sand,
calling him
by all of his names.
Her breasts burnt red,
defending the right
of women to go bare-breasted.
The hippies,
clattering magic and bells,
scattering in all directions.
The dunes,
spanning an unbearable horizon,
rising each morning clear
of all footsteps, their spines
paper crisp, each grain
of sand weighted and in place.
The lost boy
who wouldn't be gathered
in the wing of the emu
and raised to speak
a wild language:

his death
in a dream would be
perfect as an egg,
silent as a shell
in which the sea can not be heard.
William, Willow, Will,
fingers and toes counted,
all in their place,
asleep in the sun:
they crowned the man who found him
Oberon, king of the fairies.
And gathered in their vans and drove on
into the desert.

Eucla Beach

My grandmother loved to walk, along rivers, in the hills, on beaches.
To walk connected her to herself, to a world unjoined
from its joined-up dots, unpicked from human claims.
She would have loved it here,
on the 'treeless' Nullarbor, or 'Oondiri' (the waterless).

She and her husband, and my three-year-old mother,
leaving England like leaving the planet, carried
my feral seeds, their future – empty, perfect, unknown.

Sea laps towards me like the breath of another,
and draws itself back to wherever I might have been.

That stylish couple in their twenties, married for the child,
escaped their wartime upbringings, coalfed living-rooms,
with a strange defiance (bugger it, let's go to Australia) –
sailing in past the semi-white cliffs of Bunda, limestone
that sludged here fifty million years or so before them,
to a narrow city, a 'teeming sore', the bland asbestos house,

now vanished. Not to populate (one child only, she'd have six);
but to drink sherry, take arty photos of themselves, the back fence,
the crow, the powerlines. Or drive in the country, gaze at fields
purple with Paterson's Curse, 'equal to anything in England'.
Their garden was a smogless paradise of species, pigeons, wagtails,
honeysuckers, magpies, scoffing their alphabet birdfeed.

They never lost their English accents, and flourished in a kind of desert:
free from the crimes of a nation not-quite-really-theirs.

Eucla bleeds the eye, a tourist beach without tourists,
bleaching into space. Back in the dunes, a past buries as easily
as sand moves, the swallowed telegraph station
shows only a chimney, its party gramophone sucked silent.
No ghosts. Light wins, is everywhere.

The beginning of all life or the end of it, the desert doesn't care.
Here, was it, that Sun Woman
woke for the first time, yawned and seeped into human days?

700 millennia back, a comet or an asteroid struck.
Fragments bounced off back into orbit, then recently
– was it 7000 years ago? – cascaded back. Tiny black tektites,
like the dung of space, are mixed in the spinifex.

Ravens

They don't flinch when we pass them.
Huge roadtrains thundering by
leave them unflappable,
six or seven stationed around each roadside carcass.

Their delicate beaks scissor up the entrails, string them out.
Purple-black wings (doctor's bags), obsidian grit-eyes,
staunch claws: all are un-uprootable.

From the window they form miniature cities, petty officials
meticulously filing our accidental sacrifices
that bring them to the road as to the shore
of another country.

Town

Ghost-towns, machinery
rusting in a yard, spiders glowing in their webs.
Time is ahead of us, has been and gone.

Leaving camp, before a storm

A jut of wood beneath the foot.
One music, then another far off,
or silence: the desert jolting the mind
with the shock of the same.
The ground at eye-level
planting out and outwards:
grubby white,
pink, glassy, milky; amulet rocks
in the walls of the riverbed
where I squat to piss.
A child's cry balls up into
space and dissolves.
The air missive, a storm coming:
a road train shaking its neon into daylight.
The fire must be covered,
all litter collected.
We patter in ghost-dust,
skim around
squinting for signs, blessings
(eagles, rainbows, anything!);
awed, bowed down, spooked,
darting like children in the empty
house of someone
who may or may not return.

Night-driving

The highway strung between borders, naked and whole
as a planet. Stars and comets, rumours of UFOs.
Mauvish lights flash on either side of us. Thomas, awake,
suddenly trusting himself, is the driver, lurching the Bedford
from the storm at a trick of the keys. He trembles in the warm
pink of his body like an infant dreaming,

all his confessions – middle-aged flight from home, his
shouted-down need for a laundromat – swirling inside him.
Riveted, he leads the convoy as if it were his life just grasped,
four vans behind him. The road sheer as the path of the whales
who sailed straight down from space to shape
the plains with their bodies, their starry visions

rolled in sand and crusted in salt. I rattle by the door,
perched on a jerry-can; the edge of the road eroding darkness,
small eyes nibbling. He trembles in his roly pink warm body,
in the public servant of his mind. Time and night and day
hurtle by us, through us, in a clear wind, and then: the border,
morning, two rainbows, a wedge-tailed eagle circling us!

Bunda Cliffs

The shelved-in sea hived with diagonals,
verticals, horizontals, slabs of sleek water
ferrying hazes of air in its crystal,

vapouring the desert's tongue.
We funnel blue glimmers, personless gases,
far-outness pouring in to the breath,

our own power just enough to keep us
from billowing out like kites. The cliff
props itself up, its piles of age and buried faces,

dark water churns below, life-bringing whales,
their arched mouths never shut,
swilling plankton in the dream of their species

not singing, silent
as the geckoes flicking between crevices;
accessible only by suicide.

Horizon and edge unspool each other.
Nullarbor rotting behind us, strips of new blood
in tufty fringes of spear grass,

a happy-wandering campervan
zooming in the carpark. A man
hobbles out towards the edge

with his camera, his wife sits tight
in the driver's seat, not glancing up,
knitting as if she could pause

no more than time could. As if she knitted
the fabric of a species that might
at any moment unravel –

its brain-tucked memory, its scrawly
life in a particle of sand, a primal gust
of helium and hydrogen.

Dance

This edge, the soul's theatre.
Their bodies dance, they tip-toe
to the edge of the cliff, the Bight.
They dance and shimmer on the bright rims
of their souls, snake-charmed out of themselves
by the air of illusion, blistery conjurer.

Eyre Highway

The desert has no centre, is all centre.
The road, cut straight through it, racing, fierce
as rapids, is all-powerful, its god-trucks belting out ks,
animals dying of speed, mallee whirling like dervishes –
but it cannot cut the desert in half, cannot be
its sole vein, heart, pathway.

Road shimmers and melts,
shrinks like a scab, like a river in drought,
swallows heat, glints like a magnifying glass
tilted to get fire from the sun.

Road goes through instead of in,
road blinks and is gone.

Small human rubbish bins
are stationed along it for our litter.
Daniel walks there, diminishing, a banana-skin
in the pot-boiling light, the bitumen
resting as we rest in the ditch with the hum
of a truck coming near, bringing its storm,
its slap of speed, a kite snapping.

Road covers, like a long grave, the foot-paths
of explorers who wandered in
to the white of the eye,
its burning-point where water
doesn't answer, the tongue
can't ask its question.

Kangaroos

The idea of a desert is somewhere beyond our little camps.
Some kangaroos watch until I get very close, their nucleic eyes
slipping down the other side of the incline,
their slow heavy silent mechanical
hindquarters clenching, unclenching them away.

All along the roadside their bodies lie open like fruit,
stiff legs in the air, the puddling fur going khaki in lifeless grass,
a long fence of skulls saying *do not enter this desert . . .*

But each death looks momentary, one wrong leap against
thousands of right ones; thousands of hours
lived hurtling through space with no notion of obstacle.

Quick-jumps, paws dipped, their tail-sailing
walloping gait a conqueror's dream, their gestures
so almost-human, almost-comical, we might think
they saw themselves in us, answered us with *like, like.*

Always turning to leave, wider to go –
they emerge in dissolving light as if they carry
the Earth in their skins, as if they are the land they inhabit . . .
it stares at you through them, looks through you
in the shared-breath stillness, their telepathic here now
group hesitation. As if something's deciding
whether to let you in, or through. As if there was an opening,
a closing. Then turning away again, loping off
into that open where death stands to one side (you imagine)
and each leap is a leap into deeper life, deeper possession.

Cactus Beach

35 descended, with colours and music.
35 of us lit up a small cove with bright-coloured dusty torn clothes,
with breasts let down like sandbags,
with penises swinging.

Two children set down, quickly resumed their childhoods
(in each new patch of grass, assembly of rocks and trees).
One climbed up the soft cliff, bare hands and feet, while a man
(not his father) looked on in terror.

The old man (witch doctor) found his grotto up the hard cliff.

The new fire was lit with the still-smouldering coal of the last
carried in a tin of whitest ash.

The jugglers juggled oranges, sticks, their shadows, the sunset.

The women went diving for mussels, sea-sponge tampons.

The man from Canada who only wanted quiet laid himself naked
in the shallow rock pool on the beach around the corner.

I sat with the small ragged man who had no luggage
but a trumpet and cello
(trumpet for morning, cello for night),
wore a black cloak or a brown one.

His teeth stained and thinned, he said
you can have my toothbrush, I haven't
used it in years . . .

He climbed to the clifftop at dawn, we woke
to his trumpet.

When he tore off his rags and ran into the sea, we all ran
in after him.

Beyond us was a jetty, a shark net, milky still water
that remembered the blood of a young boy.
Further out, the alpine peaks of whitest sand dunes.

The desert looked on, changed nothing.

From Munich

i.m. my grandmother, Vivian Johnston, 1933 Staffordshire – 2001 Adelaide

Strange to pass through a city as through a lens.
It isn't whole – I can't see it whole –
a shop display-window, everything fur,
animal or bird, steely-eyed mannequins,
people streaming past in furs.
The city glued back together, the marionettes
in Marienplatz kicking their legs;
dislodged from time, inventing time
as she – just-vanished – seems everywhere.
She didn't entirely want to be remembered.
No grave, no plaque;
her memories, freed from her head,
swarming in mine, or some of them:
the child I was who sat on her knee
and the child she was in blackout Stoke-on-Trent
step awake, two slippered ghosts,
past houses blasted to rubble and bones
or three-walled like stage-sets.
A clock on the mantle ticking, grown-ups
alive on the footpath, marvelling in the daylight
How could we have painted the kitchen that colour?
Then her own bedroom ceiling crashed open
to the night where we both dissolve
Mother – it's snowing on my bed! – Well move the bed!

     She bared her teeth, bit my foot,
snapping my vacant stares, my
(she thought) anger at being. The bleaching heat
of Adelaide, the hills there visible from her house,
puddled with lights. White lives drifting
and folding around pegs, my 'head-in-a-basket',
a pottery-class disaster, gleaming
pink and yellow in her loungeroom.

The eye, wild as a bomb, explodes on the present,
its glittering air washed of the dead,
the neither-soul-nor-body light
of a city moving into its future . . .
How it is to glide (she sailed)
from one half of the planet to the other,
a full moon floating on the rounded window,
face to face with you anywhere on earth
like a watchful parent. She feared
coming undone: couldn't will herself safe.
Our 'psychic connection', half game, half true,
sparked in the silences, her depressions
and mine. I imagine it unbroken.
Even in Munich, a place removed from Adelaide
as one mind from another: strangers
folded up in themselves, mutely intelligible
as shades tripping out of the dust
of a once-vanished city
muttering along the ordered snow and ice
of the Englischer Garten. I can't be certain
death satisfies her. She glints and promises
in the small sphere of the watch that was hers –
Of course I knew you were looking for one
– Think of me when you wind it!
She died alive, her last words on waking,
It's not a dream, is it?

31.12.01

A Likeness

1

He thought she told him nothing, because he told her everything.
In his painting she balanced a porcelain cup on her head;
Francis Bacon, his reconfigured father, stared out above her.

His self-portraits were rainy ghosts, the nose always larger
than in life. Angels plagued him; he drew one, splayed
from wall to wall like a pinned butterfly

thinking *If-it's-not-sublime-I'll-burn-it.*
She trawled for a phrase that would slam like a guillotine
and slice their knots, return them to their almost-childish love,

                                                    and so on.

2 *Victoria Parade*

His body seemed unconvinced
of its arrival. Revenant,
he stood, marooned in a red
velvet gown, pressuring
the darkness like a cat,
the windows wide to let him go,
the marble cold fireplace
half lit by his foreign heat, his
eyes that tried to draw in
the past, the future, and exhale,
through hers, a vision
that confounded.

But their foiled speech was a body
ruled by madness. His teeth
jostled one another like soldiers
interlocked at the elbows
to form a wall,
his face cracked as parched ground
came briefly alight with tears –
he sank it down into the bedclothes.
She gathered him up, his ear-lobes,
his half-starved lips, wove
her tongue between their voices –
the frail, unplayable song
as once it must have sounded
in her undiminished ear;
and that fevery expanse
blew in, its sailable winds.

A being of nobody's creation
there he slept
in the wintry light of curtainless windows
rattling with fresh traffic
a morning on his cheek
his lips pressed stern
as if breath would take him.

3

Impossible to say it is over. She was an angel
sprung from a tree, a monster who took the house key,
who couldn't recover his beauty from the waste.

His weight in memory – a gift she could neither keep
nor return. Each other's muse: she'd meant
to make sense of what can't, beginning and end.

Who is this said to? In Brunswick Street he stood and waved,
recognition breaking its dumb light across his face,
a ring surfacing, untarnished from a grave.

4   *Cobram*

Impaled all day by the tiny twigs of a hundred pear trees,
sweated by four crates of unripe pears,
their stalks not to be broken . . .
A sleepless argument wrung their words and necks and they
traipsed through airy dust to the Murray, sullen as family.

The long road squinted, and trucks flashed past their thumbs,
the prickly-pear like so many hands held out by the roadside.
In Cobram, nothing to think to free themselves,
the main street a maze of stillness. A word or a name
painted on a rusted van said too much.

Each morning herded out to the fields in gangs
led by amazonian women – whom the men,
the 'gun pickers', feared. The leader had said to him
are you a clown? his fruit-picking clothes too big;
he'd giggled nervously, shouted *No, an arTISTE!* –
reeling off into the panic, head full of meanings.

Downstream, a couple from Holland
effortlessly piled up fruit, scrambling
in and out of trees, innocent as monkeys.
She perched in their rocky bed (no tent!)
book pointing to the river.
Why didn't he say he couldn't swim?
She surged towards him, foisted him up,
shouted through water's blind tug;
and with some monstrous, unknown strength, ferried them
to the prickly islet, a foot from the shore.
The childish thankful gaze, a luminous moth
hovering around her temple. She couldn't
look at him. She looked at the trees.

A wall of muscular ghost gums, shedding their splintery
daylight, they seemed to double, ribboning
white and dark. A pulseless quiet
on the river, their naked bodies
crouching in mud;
between them the weaving
capillaries of promise hardy as coral
that wouldn't survive a sea storm.

Bookmark

i.m. Robert Creeley

Essen, levelled by
housing blocks
four storeys high

its people
prop up windows
with elbows
and look out
on rebuilt streets
known or strange

and stop in space
they don't fall

but float in the place
of those who did
they are the living
adrift from the dead

breathing their own
invisible souls
into the present
as a reader
breathes into the word shells
a writer has left

Nursery Song

Under her wig, brown as of an old
store mannequin, she tucked the bills
unsewn from the mattress – where did
you hide her voice? and the jaw
creaked slightly at the asking. She
wasn't quite in there, but you clung
to her ankles nonetheless, and her legs
rocked on their stilts, the skirts
opening like the curtains of a pantomime,
her laughter
        always coming at the end to signal
the smaller one, the wood-cutter who rides in
on horseback to burn her garments and skin,
        she rises, she is
        the puppet of our tribe, she is not
the goddess but the mother reconstructed
out of dentures, gold rings,
pieces of our trouble. She ungirths
her great voice – like a rusty fish-hook
lying in the grass, it draws out
our most rancid memories, her breasts,
like punctured udders,
squirt milk in multiple directions,
fresh and white. The promised land
thrives beneath her skin, her seasonal resurrection
brings on the usual shower of god-rain:
        unkillable effigy, she heaves
her smouldering bosom and sings!
        yoked, we share her, endlessly igniting
never fruit. Clasping
her powdery head in our hands, foot
and neck we love her and bodily hold her,
fearful lest she shatter.

Voyage

for Clifford and Catherine Overton

The man who suddenly saw his five-year-old daughter
ascending the ski-lift alone and unbuckled
was not Dedalus, nor she Icarus.

She passed him as she passed the sun.
He could not tear his eyes away, and prayed
she wouldn't see him; one glimpse of his fear

might bring her tumbling sixty feet.
So he stood, a scarecrow of distraction on the snow
and dream-like she sailed up through blind-white cloud.

For Dorothy

i.m. my grandmother, Dorothy Marchesi, 1908–2005

Ninety-six, and nearly dead of a snapped hip, but they bob
in the shrinking pool of her vision, her seven children.
They peer into her as if into a plug-hole, grasp at her life
where it trembles in her moth-eyes, and sprawling ears;
and mouth that rustles words to each, as if to let them know
they are known. She sleeps and turns them over to themselves.

The shared ghosts that can't be elbowed away
bind them in the hospital corridor. They re-banish
a dead-banished father, 'a man who could not carry
his burden in life', who was war-shocked –
his violence simplified all memory of him.
A painter of watercolours, he carried the 'creative'

glimmer in the genes, and fled periodically to Melbourne
from the flat unblinking pragmatism of Adelaide
and family; and died there. She couldn't pay
to return the body; he's buried (she said) 'in Flemington',
where there is no cemetery. The fierceness of lack,
always the same old enemy, unchewable meat

in her children's teeth, all escaping school
to rope sausages, froth milkshakes in long tin cups,
grow businesses miraculously as beanstalks.
Her adopted eldest daughter fills like concrete
the bedside chair, spilling a lemon spawn
of knitting for her own great-grandchild.

Through the glamorous atrium and up
the twin steep escalators then down the dingy inner stairs,
her ward at the end of the crackling
yellow-tape path. She peters in the small
web of her breath, strung to the fuzzed
elms outside, the puckering fluros above,

the alien titanium hip sleeps in her body, immortal,
the morphine insects dance on the walls.
Cheeks white as cuttle on the plastic-sheathed pillows,
she fish-stares upward, steely and appalled
as the grim, red-haired single-mother-of-eight
who never smiled in photos, and at seventy married

a forty-eight-year-old man who failed to notice her age.
They drove to country music discos, their silver-furred
space-age garb shuffling them back and forth
in the slow revolving light. By his quick death at fifty-nine
she was polished as a river stone, a woman
shunning all further men. The family

freeze themselves around her and endure each other
as if none now can change. My father and uncle
dream of living to be her age, and cheating age,
and they want her mythical motherly strength,
theirs to inherit; not the frailty
and dependence she bundles into with steady eyes,

but the furious hands, wheeling their twelve-year-old
brother in his hospital bed on trains, down windy streets
in the last stages of leukaemia. They watch as she becomes
less than they can grasp, and leaves like a word
on everyone's tongue the fragile pink of her non-kiss,
her body pure milk beneath the gown.

Lady's Informal Robe

Qing Dynasty, 1890s, National Gallery of Victoria

Paisley, butterflies, grasshoppers, flowers –
and in the robe's red centre, small settled globes
of embroidered trees; threads of a self-contained
world, or a heart nothing ever burst out of.
Staid chair nearby, no-one's to sit on. On the wall
is the portrait of an ugly official whose
dress simply happened to match hers,
the dead so easy to throw together.

The gown shakes itself in the draught, a silk
flapped free of its wearer. Cool as a skin,
it rustles lightness, unbreachable grace:
we'd long to fit it as the foot longed to fit
the tiny slipper, and halved and quartered itself.

Karri Forest

near Manjimup, Western Australia

It swirls you in its poem, slows the protester
chained to a tree, the logger chainsawing his
future together, to the pace of chessmen,
in a battle that must be waged one-tree-at-
a-time on moral ground stodgy as mud.

Sepia tangles of tree-waste, the earth
lifting its bare prickly head: what to do
with all this light – is it light? At night I walked
into the forest (what remained). Moonlight
brazened on the scabby wood, red Xs

scrawled on bark; already there, the dead tree
across my path I couldn't seem to cross,
the corpse I killed and buried and forgot,
in a dream that wakes and circles, always
convinces, as one's guilt always feels right.

Ideas of Order at Point Lonsdale

The ageing pier croons and sways,
    a tied-up boat, entirely absorbed
in water's undecided plunk
    against its sides, at any moment
ready to unmire and carry
    out to fields of shadeless glitter some
scarcely fazeable fishermen;
    and children, twitching in the fresh air,
goose-bumped, beaded with salt water,
    balancing, climbing on the railing,
their faces wholly kaleidoscoped,
    who hurl out an empty line and shout
to a sea-monster half-aroused
    below; but the line flings back again,
a spider fleeing its own web,
    forced by the hide-and-seeking stranger
wind, and the smallest bumps her head
    on the rail and cries. All three watch as
water turns serious, frowning
    and furrowing into its first depths.
Hooked parrotfish swing, flashing their
    lively mutilated corpses, fish
after fish seeps through the cloudy
    eye of its brother – sea unfolds its
never-to-be-lifted skirt, the
    children, silenced with real bait, crouch tense
as lovers, fighting off a slow
    descending weariness of no named
inheritance; a deep whale yawn
    like someone's or no-one's tired mother's
drops into early dusk, the boy
    startles, looks out past the others, his

chest puffing out armour, the sock
    slipping round his ankle; wave on wave
with toothless grin and snarling beard
    rolls in its bed and visibly dreams
of a fish as spry as his hand,
    green as his green eye, arch as his foot.

And each holds fast, none drift, although
    the wide black ships thin to their pin-lights,
and the young moon goes spritzing off
    to haunt another planet: the prize catch,
the salmon that fought so all lines
    tangled, dragged back and forth by the mouth,
lies in a long string bag, slung low
    round the elephant leg of the pier,
forgotten even as dinner,
    alive, pushed by the sea in and out
of shadows, a mascot dancing
    alone, to an old, bleak music of
rising water, its silver scales.
    Stiff in the breeze, the moth-eaten man
near my elbow clings to his rod
    that seems to be steering him home, or
into the shade of a fixed star
    hidden out of sight. Time like a barge
moves in and quietly chafes through
    a last hour's stillness. Some people pass
with murmuring children and clanky
    buckets. He shivers like a hatchling,
and trip-traps of feet grow louder
    then suddenly cease, the boards humming
above cold sea. What makes him stay?

The sea surges on its indigo
    as if to shove us back to land;
but his dilate eye is blazing with
    outward-seeking light as ships glide
in and blow their horns to the houses
    nestled behind the cypresses,
and a bark canoe scrubs down to a leaf,
    on waters where North creeps behind
clouds and changes into South. A large
    crab skitters air on the end of
his line, two eyes looming, wakeful, hot
    spears, scrambling to pinch; with a twist
of the arm he sends it hurtling back.

'The Sound of Work' (*p 32*): Part 1 revises and expands my poem 'Public Service', originally in *The Simplified World*. In Part 3, the line 'our human idea of having a Self' is from Auden's poem 'The Aliens'. In Part 6, the final four lines are written loosely in imitation of the ending of Rilke's poem 'Der Tod' ('Death').

'Woman and Dog' (*p 53*): the final line is a turn on Elizabeth Bishop's well-known line.

'To William Drummond at Hawthornden' (*p 55*): the quotes are from Drummond's *Conversations*, which record his fellow poet Ben Jonson's visit to him at his home, Hawthornden Castle, in Scotland, in the winter of 1618-19. I was a resident Fellow of Hawthornden Castle International Retreat for Writers for a month in 2008.

'Spring' (*p 68*): much of this poem is a pastiche of altered phrases from British *Vogue* and *Harpers Bazaar*.

'Ode to Coleridge' (*p 69*): Coleridge's 'Dejection: An Ode' counters his friend Wordsworth's idea that Nature's fostering of the imagination can be a stay against depression. The quotes in italics here are from the final book of Wordsworth's *The Prelude*.

A few changes have been made in poems from my first two books, as follows. Four poems are omitted from *The Simplified World*. The numbering in 'Southbank' (*p 108*) is altered by the cancellation of the original second section. 'St Kilda Night' (*p 54*) and 'From Munich' (*p 130*) are adjusted titles. Slight alterations have been made in 'Pacific Gulls' (*p 100*), 'Grave' (*p 104*), 'A Likeness' (*p 132*), and 'St Kilda Night'.

This Revised Edition (2018) of *A Hunger* omits one poem and makes changes in 'Meeting' (*p 5*), 'Ode on Love' (*p 6*), 'On Time' (*p 9*), 'Pearl Diver' (*p 31*), 'The Sound of Work' (*p 32*) and 'The Relic' (*p 40*).

PUBLICATIONS IN PRINT FROM JOHN LEONARD PRESS

2006
A bud *Claire Gaskin*
Cube Root of Book *Paul Magee*
Ocean Island *Julian Croft*
The Passion Paintings: Poems 1983-2006 *Aileen Kelly*

2007
Vertigo | a cantata | *Jordie Albiston*
The Incoming Tide *Petra White*
Letters to the Tremulous Hand *Elizabeth Campbell*
Man Wolf Man *L K Holt*

2008
Poems 1980-2008 *Jan Owen*
White Knight with Beebox:
New and Selected Poems *Peter Steele*
Growing Up with Mr Menzies *John Jenkins*
Therapy Like Fish: New and Selected Poems *Marcella Polain*

2009
Collected Poems *Vincent Buckley; ed. Chris Wallace-Crabbe*
The sonnet according to 'm' *Jordie Albiston*
White camel *Morgan Yasbincek*
Pilbara *Mark O'Connor*
Marriage for Beginners *Catherine Bateson*

2010
The Simplified World *Petra White*
Patience, Mutiny *L K Holt*
Phantom Limb *David Musgrave*
The Gossip and the Wine *Peter Steele*

2011
Error *Elizabeth Campbell*
and then when the *Dan Disney*
Young Poets: An Australian Anthology *ed. John Leonard*

2012
Braiding the Voices: Essays in Poetry *Peter Steele*
Cumulus: Collected Poems *Robert Gray*
Collusion *Brook Emery*
Recurrence *Graeme Miles*

2013
Walking,: New and Selected Poems *Kevin Brophy*

2014
Stone Postcard *Paul Magee*
A Hunger
with The Simplified World *and* The Incoming Tide *Petra White*
Keeps
with Patience, Mutiny *and* Man Wolf Man *L K Holt*

2018
A Hunger (*Revised Edition*)
with The Simplified World *and* The Incoming Tide *Petra White*